BALZAC'S HUMAN COMEDY

World Literature: A Global East-West Series

First Printing, 2025

GEW HUMANITIES GROUP

BALZAC'S HUMAN COMEDY

CONTENTS

INTRODUCTION: A MASTERMIND IN CONTEXT

The Historical Context of Genius

It is necessary to dissect the historical and sociopolitical atmosphere surrounding the literary genius Honoré de Balzac. His life began in 1799 in Tours, France, where he would have witnessed an era filled with significant political and social transformation. After the French Revolution, France underwent lasting changes as powerful institutions were removed and rearranged to mirror liberty, equality, and fraternity. In addition, the rule of Napoleon Bonaparte created a large cloud of uncertainty across Europe. Against that backdrop, Balzac's life was filled with an unquenchable zeal to unravel complex layers of human existence through his writing. This compels us to ponder the emotions captured in his art, which were as complex as post-revolutionary France. Balzac's scope of seeing the world was influenced by the era he lived in. Unsurprisingly, his insight into social changes, class conflicts, and the general state of humanity is deeply rooted in the history he experienced. Quite literally, it seems that Napoleon wielded his power just so Balzac's words could flow seamlessly, and the world could witness his unparalleled literary brilliance.

To fully appreciate Balzac's profound insight into the intricate details of human nature, it is crucial to consider the prevailing economic and cultural context. The burgeoning Industrial Revolution, social class divides, and the rise of the bourgeoisie were all potent themes in his works. A closer look at Balzac's life and works within the context of these social and historical events will help us grasp the driving force behind his writing. Just as his life was a canvas on which the complex dynamics of dreams and societal change in 19th-century France played out, his works also capture the interplay of dreams and reality. His literary contributions are profound enigmas, and a deep dive into the historical context of his works is essential to fully appreciate Balzac's legacy.

How to Understand a Literary Prodigy

In Balzac's case, it is most accurate to say that he was a literary prodigy because of how effortlessly he charmed people through intricate storytelling. He deeply understood the fabric of human nature. He lived through the chaotic time of post-revolutionary France, which undoubtedly shaped him in one way or another. For a man deeply interested in drama, his life directly served as the foundation of his fantasies. It allowed him to build and repay deeper societal tensions and norms.

Balzac excelled in literature because of his ability to effortlessly separate the mind from the body and expose all its complexities, good or bad. His insight into what makes people who they are allowed him to produce a remarkable body of work that spans many years. Balzac's perspective toward humanity was much more than just on a surface level; he participated in the intellectual and philosophical discourse of his time, blending different ideas to achieve his goals in writing. He had such an insatiable appetite for knowledge that he devoted himself to studies and produced narratives that were unmatched even today. This type of thinking enabled Balzac to expand the boundaries of literary realism and set the standard that no other writer had ever been able to do or maybe even surpass. His writings defeated boundaries set by literature while diving fearlessly into human passion, ambition, and ethics. In addition, there is much more to what Balzac does as a visionary than just literature. He constructed his stories based on his arguments regarding economics, politics, and sociology, making him more sophisticated than any other author.

Balzac's detailed exploration of power relations and the social order served as an exemplary milieu in which his characters excelled and failed, granting the audience direct access to the vibrancy of society. While we commence this endeavour to deconstruct the mastery of Balzac, we should, at the onset, recognise some of the changes wrought by his work in the sphere of literature and the still contemporary communication of his stories. In this exploration, we seek to interpret the depths of his artistry in the hope that it will provide us access to the mind of a literary master.

Objectives and Scope of the Book

The objectives and scope of this book are based on the critical appreciation and analysis of Honoré de Balzac's contributions to literature, philosophy, and social criticism. This book intends to analyse Balzac's life and works, as well as his contributions to the literary and cultural worlds. Through research and analysis, this particular book seeks to understand deeply character construction, narrative structure, and themes Balzac had in mind, demystifying the art of Balzac in the process. In addition, the scope focuses not only on his life and work.

This book takes a comprehensive approach to understanding Balzac's life and works. It delves into his life surroundings, paying attention to the socio-political systems of the world, primitive philosophy, and the artistic movements of his time that influenced his thoughts and creations. By situating Balzac within the context of his time, it demonstrates the break between his works and the culture of nineteenth-century France. The book also looks at Balzac's works from an interdisciplinary perspective, using the lenses of literature, philosophy, sociology, and art history to better comprehend his heritage. By applying an analytical approach, it captures Balzac from numerous angles and from previously unexplored modern academic vantage points. The ultimate goal is to reveal and make available to the readers the finest details of Balzac's life, rich imagery, thoughts and emotions, and his profound understanding of humanity.

Examining The Concept of an Intellectual Milieu

Examine the sociology of culture once more, this time in relation to Balzac's emergence as a creative powerhouse. The sociological and anthropological factors that led to this phenomenon were indeed decisive.

The complex socio-political landscape of the 19th century, influenced by modern revolutions, industrial innovation, and the development of new ideologies, played a significant role in shaping Balzac's literary career. Alongside the French Revolution, a significant event of the time, a large group of thinkers, writers, and artists arose in Europe, hoping to make sense of these political currents. Balzac, too, was deeply impacted by the socio-political climate of his surroundings, which shaped his understanding of the world and his literary vision. He was heavily influenced by philosophical debates and artistic salons, which crafted ideas that assisted Balzac in forming a vision and developing a strong narrative. The blend of romanticism, fervour, Enlightenment ideals, and the newly formed scepticism allowed the literary masters of the centuries to contemplate the multi-faceted human condition.

Balzac’s work explores the intricate interplay between culture and imagination in his world. This extends beyond his writing to the entirety of his life and experiences. This section focuses on the cross-cultural current that defines Balzac’s worldview. This analysis of Balzac reveals an interesting interplay between culture, imagination, and some of the most politically volatile times in European history.

The term “creative era” refers to the period between 1850 and 1960. Condensed into just over a century, so much has been accomplished in the field of art and literature that it feels like a utopia of creativity. Visionary minds defined the entire period of British Romanticism, Modernism, and Postmodernism. This period is marked by an egregiously liberal form of expression and equally provocative template use. All forms of literature underwent a metamorphosis.

The continent underwent profound changes amid Europe's staggering political revolutions and industrialisation. These changes inspired many writers, artists, and even philosophers. The changes helped modern society focus on the essence of human life and raw emotions. This spirit of creativity deeply resonates with how Honoré de Balzac and his contemporaries approached their art pieces. Balzac’s need to feel and understand his own emotions and express them through art puts him at the forefront of his contemporaries. When observing this era, one can’t help but think about the tradition and innovation that took place within the realms of art. The same art that was crafted during a transformative period in Europe. Through Balzac's emotion-infused artwork, we learn to appreciate literature for the interplay of civilisation, history, and cultural memory. We question the place and power of art and, more importantly, how deeply literary realism penetrates humanity's thoughts and shifts cultural heritage's tides.

Here, we delve into the contextual specifics of a period when we experienced a rare merging of age-old tradition and new futuristic ideas, which gives us insight into the implications of this merging on culture and society as a whole.

The New and the Old: A Divide Reconciled in Art

It is important to note that, about their art, writers were operating within a paradigm of political and social change, much like Balzac's contemporaries. There was a new way of narrating stories that diverged from the preexisting norm. The fundamental challenge within this transformation was the preservation of the old way of storytelling. This balance showed that elegance and pioneering creativity are not mutually exclusive, which were quintessentially Balzacian. Some of the most striking ways he accomplished this balance was by blending realistic human life with fantastical and imaginary elements. He transformed the daily life hurdles of his characters by sprinkling some magic on them and, in doing so, captured the world's attention. Through this, Balzac clearly pointed out that tradition is not incompatible with innovation; it can nourish and revive it and, via extension, define conventions within literature.

Furthermore, focusing on the details and the essence of human behaviour shows that Balzac also deeply respected character-building and plot archetypes while revealing new avenues to understand humanity in literature. Through his works, Balzac captured the complexities of human feelings and social relations and revealed the coexistence of innovation and tradition and how those opposing forces can blend to create astounding pulsations of storytelling. At its core, integrating innovation and tradition in Balzac's corpus reveals his thrust to divert from traditional forms of artistic expression while maintaining their respected support. His works, ordered in phrases, intermingle the established realities with the invented ones, creating a route for other writers to follow. In this way, Balzac inspires modern authors to find an equilibrium between established norms and new creations through his unprecedented means. This is why he stepped into the mist of innovation with great courage, knowing that it would only serve to amplify the intricacies of literary tradition and deliver balance in the tension between invention and civilisation.

The Making of a Cultural Icon

Honoré de Balzac has certainly carved a distinct niche for himself in the literary world, which has given him immense popularity and made him a cultural icon.

His contribution to the development of the novel as an art form is astonishing. He shifted the borders of what could even be considered literature. Balzac pioneered the novel as an art form because of the unique way he narrated stories, coupled with his profound knowledge of human beings. The time period Balzac lived in had a particular context that was important for his art. Balzac is a product of a time and a place that was changing too fast for its own good. Through the examination of the human society, politics, and culture of France after the revolution, he wrote books that profoundly affected his readers, earning him a place in history. Hence, what started with Balzac inspired other writers to depict reality in their work. His pledge to honest characterisation and environmental description in his writings was unparalleled, causing an entire shift in literature. Instead of serving as a resource for writers, literature became a means for depicting reality in an artistic form. Writers crafted their narratives based on real people and places, transforming the portrayal of characters and settings into something completely new.

With profound creativity and a touch of drama, Balzac embraced and added a wealth of depth to the plot of novel writing by examining its essence and core. He, as a figure from the cultural world, is still alive and is, even today, revered from around the globe. He has impacted almost every artistic field, from books, paintings, movies, and plays. He continues to be relevant because he was able to affect the inspiration of so many people. In the modern world, he is a testament to the fact that the story has an essential place in our society as a form of inspiration and motivation to all humans around the world, and his prose is proof of the countless human experiences he affected positively.

Building Blocks of Realism In Literature

The realism in literature that changed the world of books in the 19th century became a key component in making sense of Honoré de Balzac's work. Realism is an art that depicts mundane activities like daily living, culture, and people's day-to-day existence, and it introduced a novel form of depth to writing.

Balzac is often credited as one of the first figures in this movement, crafting elaborate tales depicting the rich intricacies of human life. Coupled with this, the blending of romantic idealism and raw truths comprised the essence of literary realism. Writers did not shy away from delving deeper into the ordinary details of life so they may be portrayed at large. For instance, in his novel 'The Human Comedy', Balzac carefully renders the details of society and gives sharp insights that speak to his realistic intent. Realism in literature shifted the 'norm' of writing as it was understood until that point, focusing more on climbing social issues, unfiltered social life, and virtually everything that comprises a society's 'gritty' reality. In doing so, it allowed readers to form deeper bonds with the text by reflecting on their own lives, which remains the case for readers today. Every emotion, every relationship, and every part of society helped shape the structure of a book intended for commentary on social dilemmas, an effort pushed forward by literary realists like Balzac. Moreover, Balzac's works went far beyond simply captivating the audience; instead, they captured the paradoxes and wonders of the world and used them as a canvas to reflect upon society.

Such an approach not only deepens the appreciation of literature but also fosters the possibility of greater cultural engagement and discussion around ethics, social hierarchy, and the idea of happiness. The value Balzac placed on truth and honesty throughout the narrative of his stories served as a benchmark for future practitioners of realism and opened the door for the incorporation of social concerns into art. The roots of literary realism represent more than just a plot; they embody a dedication to show the complexity of human life. This movement became a phenomenon that gave a voice to the oppressed, became the basis of social criticism, and served as an act of deep thinking. The study of literary realism and its influence on Balzac's works reveals the illumination of human life, the realities behind these works, and notions that exist to affect societal change.

An Overview of Influential Works

A discourse on Honoré de Balzac's life reveals that it is very much possible that his most influential works were fundamental in the creation of the Realist movement. Balzac composed a wide range of works that captured his time's ethical and social intricacies because of his attention to detail and understanding of human beings.

Trailing only 'La Comédie Humaine' in being a cultural keystone is 'Old Goriot', with Goriot's explosive and shallow relationships with his daughters being ripped to shreds and dissecting the tragedy and triumph entwined in familial bonds. The world they live in is as dynamic as the relationships Goriot has with his daughters. The girls actively participate in a society where materialism reigns supreme, sacrificing their father, their only source of unconditional love. Balzac demonstrates his peers and literature's make-believe world through the novels Old Goriot' and 'Lost Illusions'. It is an exquisite source showcasing the values and conflicts that once resonated through societies and still do today. Balzac's unparalleled expertise in embodying universal compassion and love in his narratives wins him countless praise, giving him the keen skill of illustrating the novel's themes perfectly. The contents of the series refer to the arts, illusions, and colonisation, masking society with an outburst of uncultured corruption. The Elusive Goriot is the most invigorating criticism of society's willfully blind ambition. Balzac's vitriolic work unveils the truth behind unattainable dreams. Along with painting a picture of the shambles put together by society, Balzac gives insight into the ruthless chase behind a dream, even if it is futile. No matter how vibrant or dreadful, 'Lost Illusions' serves as a reminder of our world.

In addition, 'Eugénie Grandet' is a detailed study of greed, solitude, and emotional self-suppression set in a provincial milieu, capturing, in style, Balzac's complex understanding of people in diverse situations. One step further into the innovative works of Balzac, every new step seems to add another piece to a balancing mosaic, pulsating with warmth, truths, and insights, rough and profound. The multilayered richness of his narratives knows no era, for the time-honoured agony, longing, and anguish speak to each reader, regardless of the generation.

Legacy: Setting the Stage for Detailed Analysis

The impact of Honoré de Balzac's literary legacy is far-reaching and permanently etched in this sphere. As we prepare to analyse and interpret Balzac's magnum opus, we must grasp the background and context of the world of writers and thinkers who came after him. Balzac's narratives harmoniously infuse human emotions, societal complexities, and psychological intricacies, impacting literature forever.

The commendation for Balzac's literary mastery stems from the way he depicts the human condition using different characters and settings. His examination of human wants, attempts, and goals is astonishingly relatable for people of other cultures and historical times. In addition, the precision with which Balzac captures the intricacies of human relationships and interactions positions him as an example for novice and expert writers. Furthermore, the thematic relevance of societal units, structures, and power boundaries continue to make Balzac's works useful. The division of societies, conflicts between ambition and virtue, and the consequences of strong, uncontrolled passions are well thought out and observed by him, and they are still relevant today. Rather than providing a narrative, Balzac is a stimulant for self-questioning and realistic contemplation on the human condition, highlighting his story towards nature analysis Balzac. It is essential to understand the depth of Balzac's legacy, especially before we thoroughly examine his works. His literature does not only serve as a source for gaining realism or translating to cinema but also as material for philosophical meditation, establishing an unquestionably profound impact on humanity.

In trying to detail Balzac's multilayered legacy, we advance towards understanding the literary world that transcends time and moves deep into the intricacies of life's essence. Balzac's literary significance will help us better understand the complex parameters of human life in literature.

A YOUNG REBEL'S JOURNEY TO AUTHORSHIP

Birth and Early Influences

Balzac's education gave him invaluable experience that would help his literary career. Balzac was born on 20th May 1799 in Tours, France. He was born into a family of prominent heritage. His father, Bernard-François Balssa, served as a secretary to King Louis XVI's council of state, a pretty lucrative position. The royal family must have influenced Balzac's grandiose perception of life, shaping him even at a tender age. However, his family lost all of its riches due to the French Revolution. As a result, they had to move to Villeparis. This move thoroughly exposed Balzac to the aftermath of the revolution in France. There was socio-political turmoil and rampant inflation. It was these shocking experiences in his childhood that developed a sense of empathy along with the ability to observe social situations in the gifted author. The societal chaos and power struggles Balzac witnessed in his childhood laid the foundation for his intricate future creative works. With a growing interest in academics and the hope of becoming an author, Balzac's parents enrolled him in the Oratorian College at Vendôme in 1814.

Honoré de Balzac's early learning prerequisites greatly influenced his literary endeavours and future pursuits. Balzac was born in Tours, France, into a bourgeois family in 1799. He was an extremely gifted child, and so his parents took every measure to ensure that he was well-educated in not only traditional academic subjects but also other forms of culture.

Balzac's primary focus in his studies was on literature, history, and languages. His tendency to absorb information was impressive and deeply curious, which would prove helpful in his later life as a writer. The balance of subjects covered in this range helped foster an understanding of human nature, society, and its history, which was familiar to him. In addition to academics, Balzac also studied music, philosophy, and fine arts. Ensuring these influences helped him grasp the socio-cultural environment he lived in further assisted the range of references that his literary works would capture. Moreover, the reception of different art forms shaped his understanding and interpretation of the complex range of human emotions and experiences. But Balzac's life was not free of hurdles; as he decided to pursue music and literary philosophy, his family, accompanied by society, expected him to follow more traditional career paths. The conflict between his interests and societal expectations was an interesting tenet in his life that would give birth to his rebellious nature and shape him as a writer.

To conclude, it is clear that Balzac's education served as a foundation for his exceptional abilities as a writer. His understanding of different cultures and the internal struggles he experienced during his education shaped his voice as an author and made him a forerunner of literary realism.

With Literary Aspirations Comes Creativity

At this critical point in his life, the young 'rebel' was starting to realise his literary ambitions. The realisation of the power of words accompanied the rebellious phase. As society and its literary greats inspired him, the author realised that the written word can provoke thoughts and challenge the status quo. The rebel's creative fervour gradually came to fruition during this period. By providing radical insights into the world, the author is fuelled by the desire to challenge the existing order with their words, making the urge to tell one's story more intense.

With idealistic zeal and a sense of protecting the truth, the writer embarked on a passionate mission to transform their self-beliefs and society's critique into captivating stories that deeply connect with the audience. While the writers were influenced by literature and absorbing knowledge, they were captivated by philosophical reflections, ideological activism, and artistic exploration. Terms such as romanticism, realism, and existential self-analysis kept replaying in the mind of the rebel, giving birth to immeasurable self-expression and creative freedom within the boundaries of literature. Along with those achievements came an inexplicable thirst for self-education. The rebel developed a passion for diverse literature, expanding their knowledge and improving their narration. Reading other authoritative figures served a dual purpose of motivation and assessment or imitation of those that came before. This stage of emerging literary interests came with an increased understanding of the exciting yet tricky journey ahead.

The young rebel began to appreciate how literature could change one's perspective because every crafted piece had the potential to elicit strong feelings, motivate people to think deeply and bring about a positive societal shift. Essentially, the young rebel's emergence of literary aspirations marked a tipping point in his path, as it formed a distinct line from rebellion against external forces to embarking on a purposeful journey towards novel writing, creativity, and intellectual freedom.

Repression of a Conventional Pursuit

During the young rebel's formative years, he showed great defiance towards the accepted career paths that were readily followed by his contemporaries. Shunning society's norms, Balzac's radical self-definitory journey was propelled by his relentless striving to defy societal boundaries. He left behind the expected quest of attaining a prestigious career in law or business, which were considered suitable for someone of his reputation. Instead, he set out to pursue his passion for writing and began to carve out his own path. His family and friends did not receive This leap of faith well, as they branded his expectations as illogical and unrealistic. However, in spite of all the doubts, Balzac was determined to pursue his aspirations and finally achieved the resolve to embark on an unconventional approach.

His rebellious spirit led him to take on the status quo and dismantle his preconceived notions of success. He did not buckle under societal pressure because he anticipated the uncertainty and volatility of a literary career. He pursued his passion with conviction and set out to defy the complacency of everyday life in which most people resign. He vowed to carve a name for himself in the world through his writing. This revolt against the status quo did not only manifest from his career choices; it was all-encompassing and shaped Balzac's perspective and creative mind. His defiance against society's pressure to choose from a set path in life showed his unwavering commitment to authenticity. This blatant noncompliance against social norms set the stage for his later literary work, as it charged his writing with an undaunted spirit and unsparing pursuit of truth. While Balzac took on the unconventional approach of pursuing a literary career, he faced immense obstacles and intense personal turmoil. The demanding situations he encountered became the hurdles that shaped his life and fuelled his determination to disavow conformity, branding him as a nonconformist star in the literary arena.

His defiance of the traditional routes served as the crucible in which his rebellious spirit was shattered, causing his tempering to be lost in transience, one that enabled him to reach a destiny that reshaped the world of literature for centuries to come.

Initial Attempts At Literature and Its Roadblocks

As Balzac set out to make a name for himself as a writer, one after the other, he was faced with numerous hurdles that would test his determination and resilience. He certainly faced scepticism with his first literary undertakings, and for a good reason, because the literary climate during his time was heavily skewed in favour of historical and classical genres. The attempts put forth by Balzac were very often met with criticism from the reviewers, making it next to impossible for him to earn his desired place in the world of literature. In an act of sheer defiance of the norms set by the critics, he began using unexplored narrative styles and themes in writing and was met with extreme resistance. Despite the setbacks, he continued to refine his craft. Still, a lot of financial struggle kept him from progressing and served as an impediment to fulfilling his creative potential.

His endeavours undoubtedly gave him a newfound name in the literary realm, but the appeal to fame came at a great price. Balzac was haunted by the thought of sustaining himself from his writing, and like many writers before him, he was required to walk vague roads filled with uncertainty and sacrifices.

Even after facing daunting financial challenges, Balzac remained steadfast in his passion for art by infusing his undying spirit and dedication into every piece he wrote. Balzac's unrelenting commitment to everything he penned singlehandedly portrays the courage and strength required to overcome the insurmountable challenges that confront those who wish to redefine the boundaries of literature. This undertaking, which seems insurmountable, illustrates the monumental effort put forth by a single individual and emphasises the undying spirit that defines a young radical striving for the glory of authorship.

How to Solve Financial Problems

Like many other authors, Honoré de Balzac also had difficulties in earning an adequate living. It was not until later in his life that the author managed to secure a comfortable income. Still, up to that point, his skills and drive were not adequately utilised. He often struggled with a lack of resources due to the harsh economic climate of Europe, which almost single-handedly stretched his creativity. Balzac had to deal with a tremendous amount of stress from unpaid bills and minimal resources and instead begrudgingly forced himself to settle in a state that could be considered normal. The combination of these harsh conditions with insufficient resources made it harder for him to concentrate on art, which, ironically, was the only way out left for him. He became determined to hold on to his money, adopted a bitterly realistic perspective on life, and waited for more favourable opportunities to emerge in the competitive world of literature.

Nonetheless, the condition of Balzac's finances drove him to put in the effort, maintain focus, and work hard towards his goals. With his determination and a little inventiveness, he escaped the harsh life he led outside of literature. He could support himself without much aid, whether by hustling deals or engaging in unusual activities that most writers would dream of. Balzac was able to acquire the resources he required to better his situation, no matter the means.

Moreover, the financial stresses shaped Balzac's introspection, which provided him the means to marvel at humanity's and society's disparities. The constant threat of losing everything to poverty has profoundly affected the overarching motifs of his works, like the portrayal of the working class, capitalism, societal social mobility, and the clash of wealth. Balzac's fictional works, based on his acute and sharp reality and memories of poverty, were indeed relatable, impactful, and profound. It is evident that economic struggle helped him become determined and allowed him to craft compelling and unique pieces of literature. This confluence of dire financial struggle gave Balzac insights into the unfathomably kindest part of the human soul, along with the myriad nuances of society that encompassed it. His exceptional ability to transcend his hurdles and imbue them into art without any qualms only affirms the impact he left behind.

Self-Publishing

To avoid fully committing to a career that would distract him, he self-published books to gain control over his life while not fully immersing himself in his pursuits.

Like a business magnate, Balzac turned a new leaf, addressing the challenging and rewarding aspects of publishing and marketing his works independently. His forays into self-publishing enabled him to try new ways of selling and marketing his books quickly. Balzac avoided traditional self-publishing systems and opted for a more personal touch, where he sold his works directly to the readers. He understood that print culture was shifting, and self-publishing, for the first time in history, gave writers more control over their work by letting them become their own bosses. In addressing how self-publishing would change the perception of a novelist, Balzac paid attention to the covers and the presentation of his novels. By punching self-publishing tickets and working with small, local printers, he ensured that his literary works' essence was kept intact. This method not only increased the functionality of his novels but also increased the recognition of his work and maintained the originality of his writing.

Furthermore, Balzac embraced self-publishing, which transformed him into an entrepreneur. This entrepreneurship stemmed from managing technologies that helped him reach new audiences. He was also inventive in his use of cliffhangers, where he left unresolved elements of the story to entice the audience to purchase the rest of the story published in segments. With the tension of the narrative, Balzac mastered crossing boundaries and accepting the social diversities of his audience. The ability of independent publishing transformed the industry, which Balzac, along with other forward-thinking writers, facilitated. Such acts give writers the ability to publish their works without any constraints. This ultimately provided future writers with more freedom in how they wished to communicate with their audience through literature.

Mentorship and Important Relationships

The self-declared literary insurgent, together with his order, still posed didactic mentors and critical relationships that were of utmost importance to his enviable essence of literary capital. This self-published writer drew the support of influential individuals ready to address their problems. Following his mentor's advice, the growing fame novel writer hosted and participated in conversations and debates and, when appropriate, wrote critiques, integrating new approaches into their work.

These influences have significantly changed and enhanced her perception of a story, how a character of any complexity is developed, and what themes to weave into the tale. In addition, the mutual respect embedded in these relationships fostered the development of trust and authenticity, establishing a foundation in the vast world of literature. In addition to mentors, other writers and thinkers became invaluable sources of motivation and initiated intellectual discourse essential for creativity. The environment composed of these active doers was one that inspired and welcomed the breaking of boundaries and the nurturing of new ideas and styles. Furthermore, these core associations reached beyond literature to include work with some publishers, editors, and patrons who recognised the promise of talent and critical opportunities for development and visibility. Forming productive relations with the existing youthful artistic and literary elite increased her esteem and confidence and provided crucial resources, materials, career opportunities, and platforms to reach wider audiences.

Breakthrough Works and Recognition

Recognition and development of breakthrough works garner undivided attention because they represent highly critical and sensitive phases that can establish or destroy the career-defining period of the rebellion-turned-author. The life of the emerging writer poses a paradoxical worldview in that while they revere artistic integrity exceptionally highly as a non-compromising factor, they approach bracing them towards achieving very anti-compromise marks in their career, arguably defined. At this phase, the author tries to achieve thematic and stylistic comprehensiveness; therefore, creativity reaches novel perspectives. While at the very centre—of all claiming to be aspiring authors—I am told under a genuinely novel, innovative, and original perspective. In turn, I am issued my emerging name. The author puts forth force, and readers of consequence begin enjoying this freely, agitating to claim their emerging name, for my portrayal of the novel industry perspective is laced all around.

The youthful rebel's efforts begin to pay off as the differences between him and the audience become insignificant. At the same time, he makes strides along with his colleagues, marking significant milestones in their career paths.

The author earned intense emotions from the readers through self-reflection and deep pondering of their core ways of life. There is a substantial reason why this particular work is considered groundbreaking. That reason acts as a trigger for social discourse and even participates in the ongoing dialogue of culture. That reason is also not superficial. By the author encapsulating aspects of every single person's life, it acts as a core tool for self-reflection. From this deep pondering, we are met with intense emotions which enable the author to reach a whole new status in the vastly revered literary circle, granting him a position among contemporaries. During this time, the author was able to earn a position alongside publicists, scholars, and other highly reputable literary entities, therefore assimilating to the strongholds of literature with a considerable soft spot. These prolific writers have had an immense impact on art. Because of these rapid collaborations with other renowned writers, the author's perception has changed forever. It's like a day and night difference. In the end, the award accolades and recognition all prove that the author has the makings of a luminary. Most reputable institutions of literature award the author with renowned recognitions, which contribute to their ever-expanding legacy. That is also why the author is offered honorary distinctions.

With all of these accolades piling on, the author's impact on the world of literature grows stronger. The newly emerged rebel rests in the glory of recognition and continues to evolve towards creative masterpieces, with the hope of changing the course of the literary world one day. Such efforts highlight the talent of the young rebel, proving that he can focus and master the art of authorship, thus marking the rise of unique, influential pieces of literature.

Formative And Key Achievements

Adolphe further suggests that throughout Balzac's life there are a number of moments and accomplishments that were tremendously important for the individual in question's career and life. Among these are the publishing of 'Les Chouans' and 'La Peau de chagrin' that stand as milestones as Balzac's work started resonating with the critics and the general public. Success with these pieces saw Balzac positioned as one of the most well-known authors to come out of Paris.

Moreover, his passion for observing human beings and their social interactions with one another contributed to what many deem as his most excellent work, 'La Comédie Humaine.' This project alone was grand in scope and thematic elements. It was a great work of art from Balzac's side, but it also illustrated France in great detail at the beginning of the 19th century. Besides his novels and essays, Balzac was most creative when it came to his life and social surroundings. His association with influential people such as Madame Hanska was advantageous to him in many ways, and their correspondence had a positive impact on his work. Significantly preceding that, the ability to observe analytically and the determination to refine his craft led him to produce an overwhelming volume of work, which set a new standard in the literary field. Another milestone was the establishment of his own printing house, which he decided to name Imprimerie Hono. This was incredibly significant because he could publish all of his writings without the restrictions of having to please anyone else. Thus, he was able to sell his work the way he wanted and was free to write without the stringent censorship of the publishers, which gave him immeasurable freedom. This enabled him to write in various forms and experiment with different ways of storytelling.

From this pioneering work, readers and scholars alike could appreciate the impressive character and stories etched from the Bronze Age into his foundational works. Simultaneously, as Balzac became increasingly popular, he published more works and achieved fame as a master of literature. He was able to earn such an achievement due to his dissertation, which employed a sociological perspective to accompany his imaginative view of the social world. From Balzac's creative and productive life, this period stands out as remarkable in the sense of the increased speed of his creativity, which gave birth to his lasting legacy of writers and thinkers. These insights and events summarise the essence of the most potent literary figure in Balzac's time while also describing the development of his career and the collective sociocultural intellect of the epoch.

THE GENESIS OF LA COMÉDIE HUMAINE

Conceptual Foundations and Literary Ambitions

Balzac's wish to illustrate the totality of humankind's experience drove him to initiate La Comédie Humaine. His endless faith in literature as a reflection of society's complexities led Balzac to undertake an unnecessarily ambitious project, constructing a narrative that sought to weave the experiences, aspirations, and struggles of people from different social classes into one story. This work was vast because, at its core, it aimed to explain the many-layered relationships between humans that are intertwined with love, deceit, and self-interest. To achieve such literary ambition, Balzac intended to fill the pages of La Comédie Humaine with the uttermost boundaries of human existence, replacing the contemporary fiction works' constricting standards. With a focus, he set out to use his intellect to create a space that resonates with life and encapsulates the complexities unique to humans. This was done while observing the ongoing societal change, as Balzac sought to document the change in French society immediately following the revolution.

Balzac's intention to analyse a constantly shifting world led him to merge personal experiences with cultural and historical accounts. This initiative allowed the development of La Comédie Humaine's concept to go beyond just a collection of stories, for it bore witness to Balzac's insatiable literary ambition and his attempts at creating an unmatched representation of the diverse human experience.

Important Influences and Sources of Motivation

The initial stages of creation for La Comédie Humaine, much like the other works of Balzac, were deeply rooted in the cultural and intellectual context of the period. He drew inspiration from many sources – through his life experiences and the works around him. His "narrative canvas" predecessor had origins extensively ranging from classical literature and philosophy to modern-day society. Through his intense thirst for knowledge, Balzac read the works of famous thinkers and writers like Rousseau, Montesquieu and Voltaire, who significantly shaped his literature. Furthermore, Balzac's peers, such as Sir Walter Scott and Henry Fielding, entirely shaped his literature. Their character-driven plots and new narrative styles served to steer Balzac's writing.

Moreover, the vivid intellectual context of France in the early 19th century, marked by enthusiastic discussions revolving around politics, ethics, and humanity, offered Balzac a perfect setting to nurture his perspective as a storyteller. Via engaging with his epoch's intellectual and scholarly figures such as Saint-Simon, Fourier, and Goethe, Balzac eclectically synthesised many ideas, which drove him to produce a piece of literature encompassing the multifaceted nature of society and humanity. Motivated by the Enlightenment spirit and the romantic rise in focus on the individual, Balzac embarked on his austere examination of the human experience by unravelling the complexity of human life through storytelling. During this phase of intellectual over-excitation, he received the impetus to start developing a monumental body of work that would theorise the chief themes of human experience about his imaginary world. While Balzac explored literature before him and the contemporary philosophies surrounding him, he shaped his consciousness as a writer, developing a deep sense of the interrelation between art, thought, and society.

The blend of these notable predecessors and intellectual influences served as the foundation on which La Comédie Humaine would stand. This reflects Balzac's skilful ability to use the remnants of the past and contemporaneity to carve a narrative legacy that spans many ages.

Text Structure: Balzac's Narrative Approach

Balzac's narrative approach, a testament to his endless literary ambition and vision for La Comédie Humaine, was a unique architectural framework that could accommodate the vast complexities of human society. This approach, akin to a carefully designed computer architecture, was meticulously blended with every feature of the narrative, from the complexity of human society to the world itself, to create a masterpiece. Balzac's extensive literature was built around the desire to create a complete picture of France and its ever-evolving society, filled with diverse contradictions and ethnically dominated areas. Each element individually shapes the intricate structural framework of La Comédie Humaine, and each narrative contributes separately to the human experience mosaic. Balzac adopted a sophisticated method of advancing this underlying framework through a constant set of characters, accompanying themes, and carefully controlled social settings where the action occurs.

The core of Balzac's architectural structure was the deliberate segmentation of his works into 'Scènes de la Vie Privée' (Scenes from Private Life), 'Scènes de la Vie de Province' (Scenes from Provincial Life), and 'Scènes de la Vie Parisienne' (Scenes from Parisian Life). This deliberate segmentation, akin to the careful placement of supporting beams in a tall structure, allowed Balzac to intricately weave the expanded pillars of his grand narrative. It enabled the profound and multifaceted human life experience across diverse social classes and regions within the world, while still having the entire story united under one theme. Furthermore, the story framework depicted intertextuality in the same manner that the supporting beams are interlaced within a tall structure. There was a leakage of characters from other works, echoes of experiences in different places, and common themes throughout the fictional lifecycle of Balzac. This conscious intertwining of stories ensured a web, resulting in multiple stories coexisting within a main one, broadening the literary horizon. Balzac's prose architecture did not only construct a fabulous tale. It also had an inbuilt control of the tension and the cadence, like the scheduled arrangement in a musical piece.

Each contribution by novel, novella, or short story serves as a devout note in the grand symphony orchestrated with an enthralling progression that captures the reader's imagination with grandeur while keeping the integrity of the opus intact. To sum up, the pertinacious structure of La Comédie Humaine is a testament to Balzac's revolutionary mastery of storytelling. He successfully encapsulated the human condition in his literary work by intricately fashioning worlds and personas within the spine of a single narrative.

First Concepts and Edits

Balzac's attempt to compose La Comédie Humaine was marked by drastic changes to the sketches and settling on more developed ones. The origins of this landmark literary initiative lay in Balzac's relentless indifference to the fine print and exceptional need to achieve the impossible. In the beginning, Balzac found himself battling the challenge of systematically constructing the plot elements and the myriad of characters that constitute the pillars of his magnum opus. Each draft served as a means to achieve the end, allowing him to perfect his storytelling skills.

During further analysis, much thought is placed on characteristic features and updating their ethics to develop them profoundly. A dedicated effort towards reaching the human character results in extensive, painstaking work. The deep, comprehensive traits that Balzac explored led him to scrutinise the motifs and themes of La Comédie Humaine. By examining the world around him, he transcended over expansion, necessitating effort to portray life. Each earlier draft tirelessly motivated him to portray not just underlying stories but rather the human essence. The fusion of creativity and determination transforms the otherwise ordinary story into a sharp and lively portrayal of humanity, which assists in challenging and redefining the Cordon White Set within the new Arc. This enables the wide-angle shot to be viewed, and the power of the very indecisiveness comes into play that foreshadows the vision. In aiding the idea, it does clarify Balzac's tolerance towards the mundane and the complex nature of creation. Unbound approaches towards self-limiting us allow the ideas to shine obstacles, revealing unexplored corners of nature's canvas. In doing so, every obstacle is conquered, unlocking a fresh meaning, waiting patiently for the opportunity to be uncovered.

Balzac's unwavering quest for perfection through ceaseless editing reflects the importance of persistence and self-reflection in art.

Identifying The Boundaries: Themes And Symbols

In his broad masterpiece, La Comédie Humaine, Balzac incorporated abundant themes and symbols that, in one way or another, reflect the different aspects of human life. Most importantly, Balzac imagined a distinct reality structure with an elaborate narrative in mind. He tried to represent contemporary society's good and evil, hope and despair in the bluntest possible manner. To accomplish this objective, Balzac painstakingly sought to determine the boundaries of their masterwork, not through forming the stories but rather by creating the scope of the themes that would connect them. Most prominent among the notions that lie at the centre of La Comédie Humaine is social order with all of its interdependent components: ambition and hope, love and treachery, power and vice, human toughness, and the moral paradoxes of life. These themes are presented with nuance and sophistication, which show the complexity of humanity and society in Balzac's fictional world. Besides, the overwhelming motifs of the like serve as the central symbols, which clarify the themes and make the texts more comprehensive and meaningful.

In 'The Genesis of La Comédie Humaine,' we traced the steps in the outlines of Balzac's attempts and processes as he stretched from the beginning to the early drafts and the final versions. Now, when we tackle the most critical stage of the division of novels into the novels and their integration into the frame structure, it is important to note how themes and motifs act as the glue that holds these different stories together. A study of the most manifest components and pieces of the contradictory nature as compared to reality, the charm of wealth and vice it breeds, and conflict between society and the individual shows that Balzac did not only analyse the relationships of humans to each other and the society but also the use of a family of human forces in devising their destiny. In addition to observing the human world, the bounding threads of the theme go above and beyond the mundane, engaging in deep philosophical interrogation surrounding being, happiness, and the eternal quest for identity self. Balzac meticulously illustrates the structure of the myriad of intricate bilateral human relations, the moral dilemmas of dominant characters, and the widespread social evils, thus provoking the world to ponder questions of singular importance that define the nature of humanity.

Integration of Novels: Unifying Diverse Works

La Comédie Humaine owes its existence to the integration of several novels. Balzac's ability to beautifully knit stories together is a masterful work in itself, bringing forth none other than the elevating integration of these works. These narratives are distinct, yet through the skilful Balzacian storytelling, he weaves separate lives into a single entity that reflects the gorgeous tapestry of human experience. Balzac's unique ability to unite and merge stories and characters stands out the most. Because Balzac decides to combine novels with a crossover of previously established varied characters, his readers of La Comédie Humaine receive a sequel where they get a centralised, wide-ranging depiction of France. The nad interconnections aid in deepening the fictional world and allow the readers to escape amidst the intricacies of the real world through the fictional universe that is now expansive and interwoven. In addition, the theme fragmentation of integrated novels provides readers with an equally exemplary balance, revealing the impact of those themes on La Comédie Humaine. Balzac can seamlessly delve into the intertwined importance of ambition, love, social power dynamics, etc.

As a result of these theories being interlinked, the reader is offered an overview of humanity that includes its joys, tragedies, wins, and losses. This tapestry of interrelated themes enchants the reader to think beyond the narratives because it contributes deeper meaning to individual stories, adding that humans are also interlaced with one another in their existence. Balzac's method of unifying the novels in La Comédie Humaine proved his ability to structure and pace a story accurately. Each book is a piece towards the broader scope of the collection, which is Balzac's world, and these pieces evoke interest from readers, as there is a sense of balance within the story. Various intricate crossovers and progressions of themes serve the purpose of guiding the reader through the expansive experiences inherent to humanity. In essence, these intertextual references to the rest of his works within La Comédie Humaine are proof of Balzac's determination to encapsulate society, human nature and the human condition in the vast tapestry of life. It is a mark of his incredible capacity as a storyteller and a builder of an unprecedented masterpiece that comes from intertwining different plots into one place.

As they explore the interwoven novels titled La Comédie Humaine, readers are exposed to the ability of a singular creative genius in Balzac to blend various works into one story.

Character Development: Crafting Compelling Characters

For Honoré de Balzac, developing compelling characters into a massive literary work like La Comédie Humaine was a multifaceted process of artistic deception. The characters of this monumental piece were not just figments of his imagination but rather manifestations of real human beings skillfully created to capture the different sides of humanity. Balzac takes his approach to character development a step further than category fiction. He peers into the individual's psyche, and the influence society has on them in great depth. At the core of his characters, Balzac understood human behaviour and psychology. His characters were exceptionally relatable due to the unique combination of virtues, vices, desires and fears that were characterised. Balzac was able to, through observation and introspection, give each character a sense of realism that captured the intricacies of their thoughts, emotions, and actions with such clarity. Along with that, Balzac's characters were not singular people. Instead, they were parts of a social structure.

Their identities existed as blended wholes about nineteenth-century France's cultures, economies, and politics, making them equally a fraction of the society's experience. By breaking down the struggles, victories, and defeats of Balzac's subjects into pieces of a bigger puzzle, he could emphasise the connection of individual lives to destinies as a whole through very profound lenses of the human condition. Balzac's multi-dimensional character development created a balance between oppositional traits and enriched integration, which extended to psychological complexity. His protagonists often possessed morally ambiguous traits that muddied the distinction between flat heroes and fully rounded humans. This depth of character refutation extends to challenging the boundaries of morality and virtue of society, allowing readers to dwell on the contradictions and complexities that make humanity what it is.

Additionally, Balzac had an astonishing capacity to maintain a character's continuity in development across several writings, like a tapestry joining many diverse tales into one, unmistakably more than the sum of its parts. Characters from different novels merged and developed together over time, produced and being produced by the interactions. All these pillars of relationships among characters and their growth as individuals provided for the single united being that La Comédie Humaine showed, making Balzac's literary creations rely solely on realism.

To summarise, Balzac has successfully blended deep psychological analysis, sociocultural understanding, and skilful storytelling into his fine art of character development. The figures in La Comédie Humaine surpass the boundaries of fiction as they are culturally relevant and indelible proof of the astounding intricacies that dwell within us, which speaks to Balzac's literary brilliance.

Narrative Techniques: Innovations and Strategies

An analysis of La Comédie Humaine will reveal broad-ranging themes and sharpen the reader's mind towards even the most potent undercurrents of narrative structures, which make it a masterpiece. In comparison to other authors, Balzac not only told stories but revolutionised the form of storytelling, crafting fiction, and the everlasting impact on global literature that followed. All of this stems from the unique blend of narrative strategies and literary devices Balzac applied, which remind us of the mastery behind his control over the plot, characters, and themes. La Comédie Humaine is enriched by this multi-level phenomenon, which broadens the readers' view of the depths of human nature and society. Balzac's ability to create parallel and intersecting plots within distinct pieces of literature is also one of the exceptional techniques he employs.

Moreover, Balzac's mastery of foreshadowing and dramatic irony enhances the reader's interest and history because the subtle pointers and clues make the looming tension and sense of anticipation within the stories more pronounced. In particular, Balzac's use of imagery and different settings is not only used for exposition; he puts the reader in the actual 19th-century Parisian life. Moreover, his use of psychological realism and reflective narration goes beneath the surface of his characters' minds, creating a close relationship between the reader and the character. Also, Balzac's narratives act as a lens through which an analysis or commentary on social issues can be made and thus serve as an efficient critique of the society encompassing these narratives and their careful insights into a person's psychology. Lastly, anticipation and catharsis are achieved by placing climactic events and deep thoughts toward the end of his stories. This creates a memorable and vivid sensation for the audience that is hard to forget. In short sentences, Balzac's life using innovative narrative techniques and strategies made him a pioneer and a vision that made him stand out, ultimately cementing his reputation as a storyteller. Two blinds spent in the years of his life laced his Christine's history of formless commode of human has.

Obstacles in Implementation: Overcoming Barriers of Introspection

Most challenges manifest themselves as a reality that every author must meet face to face.

The multifaceted nature of Balzac's craft and creativity certainly set the stage for barriers. Balzac's life milestones exemplified the Balzac barriers, which were intricate webs of writer's block and Balzac's creative hurdles. This segment shifts focus from milestones to the balance of effort versus outcome that Balzac might have sought while attempting to create his pièce de résistance, 'La Comédie Humaine.' Balzac was deeply passionate about his work, so he often found himself battling against the extreme demands of productivity and creative self-exhaustion. The work's thematic depth called for extraordinary planning, coherence, and character crafting. Trying to bring together all the pieces of work made Balzac question the balance between innovation to captivate readers and appeal to them. An attempt between harmony and discord, aligned and entwined in the same landscape. That balance, although appealing, was terrifying, knowing how much creative self-sabotage could happen. Balzac, stressing the need for cohesion, put forth his backward prose in the form of La Comédie Humaine. Trying to craft metaphors while solving such complex challenges was phenomenal. Still, it only places Balzac's narrative under the microscope of self-sabotage.

The unyielding attempts at perfection cultivated an environment rife with the shadows formed by the stagnation of creativity. Balzac scribed under the spectre of creativity's stagnation that beset him with cyclical writer's block during the most crucial junctures of his life. While grappling with the overflow of his ideas, Balzac faced continuous lulls of inspiration that left him stranded in an altered reality filled with nought but uncertainty and reflection. The weight of expectation, be it self-inflicted or thrown upon by others, hung like a deluge around him, which ultimately sullied every stroke of the pen. Balzac's place on the totem pole of creativity stagnated as life was compelled to shackle him, fastening self-fuelled complications to the necessity to produce era-defining literature. The merger of financial woes, nagging familial responsibilities, and the inexhaustive depths of human strife created barriers that made capturing Balzac's magnum opus nearly impossible. In an attempt to weather the storm of these syncretised dilemmas, he uncovered that creativity was rooted in the spontaneity of challenge and success. Balzac's steel resolve enabled the defiance of the continuously meshing realms of sanity and insanity, allowing the culmination of the desolate womb into reality. In their whispers, the overture of his life devoted to the ceaseless funnel of motivation is an ever-present testament to his brilliance.

Analysis and Development of the Idea

The analysis of La Comédie Humaine is receptor-dependent at every level, and over the years, it has transformed. To begin with,

Balzac's vision was deemed grand and faced both scepticism and, in some cases, resulted in ridicule, like most critics do when they realise the magnitude of tasks undertaken by someone. Combining several novels and stories within a single societal framework was a brute attempt to experiment with literature and cross what is regarded as the standard limit for fiction writing. But the moment his concentration on constructing multi-versatile characters and themes within the complex interconnecting nature of the plot was apparent, the critics began to change their minds. It is said that Balzac's approach was unheralded before so many and that La Comédie Humaine, highly regarded as a work of social and psychological pioneer insight, is viewed differently today. The change of view in the crystal explicit critique depicts the gradual decomposition of incredulity to astonishment with respect to Balzac's concept.

With time, Balzac has

been revered as one of the greatest writers in literary history owing to the mark his work left on the innovation of novels and their significance at different places and times. In addition, how this shift in conceptual interpretation has come about is equally intriguing. Ideas previously viewed through a modern lens have now been recognised due to changing sociocultural settings. The insights into power relations, human aspirations, and the intertwining of individual lives with the overarching historical processes still resonate with people worldwide. Balzac's approach to narrative construction and thematic focus has changed with time, just as critical theories have. La Comédie Humaine comprises various themes that offer infinite opportunities for scholars and enthusiasts to analyse and develop new interpretations. The relationship between critical interpretation and conceptual change highlights the vibrancy and depth of understanding in Balzac's masterwork, La Comédie Humaine, making it a fundamental literature novel.

BALZAC'S PORTRAYAL OF SOCIETY

Parisian Life and Characters

PARISIAN SOCIETY IN BALZAC'S TIME

In Balzac's era, Paris appears to be highly developed with complex class structures. The social elite was at the top, where aristocrats with boundless wealth set the country's culture and politics. Beneath them were the bourgeoisie, who worked hard to improve their social standing, doing their best to conform to the rules of etiquette and class respectability. Meanwhile, the working class was left with no option but to labour mercilessly, often under dreadful conditions, in the hope of affording a decent lifestyle. The social gap between the classes was wide enough to fuel conflicts so rich that Balzac alone could indulge in all sorts of literary imagination. Each class had its own set of customs, norms and grievances, giving a riveting depiction of a society in transition, and an author who was obsessed with detail. Balzac was capable of seeing beyond the splendour of Paris towards its underlying issues. He was well aware of the decay of manners, the disparity of wealth, and the uncontrollable desire to achieve everything humanity tends to seek, but what people are intertwined in how multifaceted society is.

The elite, the developing middle class, and the underprivileged fight to maintain control over their lives and pay the price of social mobility, which is the context that makes sense of the social order. The sociology of Paris examined in this essay goes a long way in making sense of the characters in the portrait, their struggles, and their particular motivations in the world that Balzac meticulously sculpted. Setting the analysis on the context and structure of Parisian society during Balzac's epoch helps us comprehend the underlying factors which drive his characters' behaviours and actions, thus expanding our comprehension of universal themes of longing, ambition, and even social integration which every society grapples with today.

Balzac's insightful observations

Honoré de Balzac is said to have been an inept observer and procrastinator, deeply passionate about Parisians. He did not just write about the geography and architecture of the city; he wrote about its inhabitants' thoughts and feelings as well. He was not only a passive bystander. Like other people from the metropolises, he was an active participant who used a new lens to analyse urban life and comprehend it.

Owing to his keen perception, Balzac's works are brought to life in a wonderfully intricate manner. His readers, for example, do not just read his books – they feel as if they are pacing Balzac's Paris, with its effervescent rhythm and picturesque settings. From the refinement of the imperial quarters to the crumbling squalor of the slums, Balzac sets the score to the heart of urban life in vivid detail. He does not capture the vivid landscapes alone but the dreams, challenges, and deep inner conflicts of the multitude of characters he portrays in his books. Balzac explains the horrific complexity of these social interactions through the human mind and the environment. The drastic transformations in the centre of Paris are depicted in his pieces as a collage of deep human experiences. Equally, Balzac was able to change the themes and portray different angles of the same story, enabling the context of Paris and the people living in it to be seen separately.

Ever the astute observer, Balzac captures multiple sides of Parisian society which, in the end, translates to abundant experiences for the reader. This is what makes him excel.

Describing City Life

Honoré de Balzac's focus was Parisian life and he perfects the fine details of the craft, and arranges scenes that portray urban landscapes of Paris life with great vivacity.

More than just depiction, Balzac was able to vividly describe life in Paris, its streets and its grand boulevards. One could recreate in their imagination the time period with Paris's vibrancy in the nineteenth century because of the precise details captured by Balzac. However, he did not solely consider urban Paris as a picturesque background. Rather, he infused it into the intricate motives of his characters' plots. This skill is now widely appreciated and was first apparent in his writings about the aristocracy's salons, powerful working-class markets, and dark but life-filled curious alleyways. All of these places are brought to life through Balzac's language and they serve as evidence of his remarkable talent. The astonishing skill, combined with the rest of the imagery, made his work feel as if his audience was truly in the scene, allowing them to experience a completely different time and place. Through these urban settings, one is exposed to the deep and intricate social structures, the ambition, and the self-destructive nature of humanity.

Balzac dissembled urban life in a multitude of layers bringing together particular locations with the mental and emotional moods of his characters. Especially, he analysed the contradictions between the glorious upper-class society and the dilapidated shantytowns of the lower classes, or even the aspirational tug of war in a polyarchic society. His works portrayed the elegance and the savagery of the socio-economic reality, which is precisely why these epochs enjoyed such popular appeal. In an effort to elaborate his stories, Balzac devoted an extensive amount of attention to the details of the social structure, and in doing so, he staunchly stood up for the socio-political transformations taking place in the cities. Balzac so eloquently and invitingly describes the world in which he lived that he immerses the public in the heartbeat of society and encourages them to ponder the intricate lives of citizens in ever-changing and complex metropolises.

Social structure and character types

With regard to Paris, the work of Balzac's character types is detailed, since he holds particular social stratification of Paris in a deep and delicate focus which Balzac termed 'the Comédie Humaine.'

Through his characters, Balzac systematically analyses human interactions across the different social classes and the aspirations, struggles, and achievements that define a bourgeois life. Each character transforms into some complex element or system of values that permits analysis of varied dimensions of human behaviour and social relations. The archetypes advanced by Balzac—the resolute capitalist, the self-made man, and even the jaded elite member—transform into bearers of distinct passions, ambitions, and societal-inflicted constraints. Types of Parisians blended by Balzac allow a closer examination of the intricacies of relationships and tensions in the life of a Parisian. Moreover, by merging these character types, Balzac explains the idea of competition and the coexisting supportive relations that shape the hierarchy in each society, capturing the essence of human relationships and the struggle for power and recognition. Emphasis on competition and the interrelations between the characters compel the reader to consider identity, ambition, and a timeless moral conflict as social relationships that are more complex than they appear, and as relationships between people with different social backgrounds.

Studying the world of Balzac's characters provides insight into our stereotypes, leading to the understanding that life is profoundly multidimensional. Readers are faced with the question of their own position in the social order, and as they study the interplay between the characters and their positions in the social order, they gain a deeper understanding of human motives and insecurities. Ultimately, the more basic tale of humanity, from which Balzac's interest in typology and character and social relations stems, is beyond the epoch in which it was created and speaks to every human's experience in the world and craves meaning in life.

A capitalist class's aspirations and anxieties

To Balzac, the capitalists represent an obsessively desired upper class, both in terms of what they hope to become and what they dread about Paris. His details capture the socio-psychological features of this social class that reveal a deep understanding of the emerging middle class during the complex period of industrialisation and urban growth in France during the first half of the 19th century. Out of all class categories, the capitalist class has a persistent upward affiliation which sustains their social ambition and zeal for economic growth.

Balzac paints the interpersonal blend between the desperate desire to be accepted in an aristocratic society and the high possibility of losing their social status point blank. Balzac, with intricacies of bourgeois ambition, examines through Rastignac in 'Père Goriot' or Eugène de Rastignac in 'Vieux Goriot'. These figures are bestowed with thoughts and physically exist in a society where ethical compromises are requirements for acquiring power, wealth, and status. The delicate paradox between struggle and the sacrifice of the agrarian capitalist class is the main critique of these works. It unmasks the imperialistic edges that unconsciously stalk anyone attempting to rise above the lower end of the Shaddock temporary totem pole. And Redistribution Vol. 1: a product of the INAIST. Furthermore, Balzac's commentary on the inner contest of the bourgeois provides a critique on the zeal to strive for social advancement that is perpetually constrained by the utmost fear of failing. The ache and fear formed by being abandoned forces the suspected middle class socioeconomically grounded, perpetually terrified, and as a result lacking opportunity. The advanced collectors on the other hand sadly without a middle ground. The icing on the cake is the collective anxiety that is caused by the feeble support of the wealth obtained.

The playwright gives Balzac's view on the attempt at sociological mobility within a stratified society. In this play, the author analyses the use and or abuse of class relations over the so-called Parisian society by the bourgeoisie social class.

In seeking to understand their claim, this entity has made, it faces the self-contradictions of its own claiming and ethical difficulties in coping with self and a new meaning in old city. Balzac shows us the self-duplication of fear and hope. With these ideas, he shows the intricacy of the bourgeois self in an almost dystopian setting. In attempting to deeply analyse the ambitions and fears of the bourgeoisie, Balzac facilitates his audience into rethinking what constitutes human composition architecture and consequently taking uncomfortable facts which sometimes go beyond time and ethnicity.

Crime and survival in the city: The hidden face of urban life

The city is a character in and of itself, the stage upon which crime and survival is set, much like the works of Balzac. As competition and crime are the by-products of a civilised world, the Archaic Parisian society is its centrepiece. And it is this urban life that Balzac attempts to tackle through the lens of transgressed Paris. While Balzac does not shy away from enumerating the details of the social fabric, he also captures the dark world of crime complete with well-orchestrated systems of organised crime existing on the fringes of civilisation. For the select few who somehow consider themselves above the rest, civilisation becomes a more complex arrangement to navigate. Some figures coming from the lower strata of class are deprived of social capital, all because of the chronic poverty that many have had to endure their entire lives. Balzac's unrestrained imagination is at work as he paints a clearer image of these crimes lacking the dire socioeconomic conditions across the globe. And with characteristic genius, Balzac integrates morality, social justice, and the effectiveness of law into the world of crime without so much as a blink of an eye.

He analyses the neglect of policing and the enforcement of legal rulings, providing a critique of the events and systems designed to manage the city, including its racism and inefficiency. By exploring the intertwined fates of crime victims and offenders, he unmasks the deeply disturbing moral issues that a society, which Balzac's soft brush would depict as a paradise, is forced to confront; a society inverted with inequality and destitution. Balzac masterfully describes the crime and the condition in which people reside, where poverty-stricken individuals crumble as society neglects them and the state crisis spirals out of control.

Consequently, he portrays social life and community relations in Paris and within the city's slums in dire pessimistic tones. Having originated from their most deprived area, Balzac suggests the social contrasts found in the less populated regions towards the uplifting features of livelier Paris cannot be endured, thus the neglected areas of the city. He dares the audience to face the horrific realities hidden under the mask of culture, civility and social manners while challenging them to confront poverty and the broken population that lies under the consequences of this society.

As a result, Balzac appears to censure civilisation metaphorically, while simultaneously describing in detail the most sophisticated and backward parts of Paris. Undoubtedly, Balzac raises some critical matters of social justice, but he also raises the most basic issue of how to help those who are themselves entangled in the web and shadows of so-called social 'evils'.

Characterisation using unique and particular literary techniques

In the manner in which Balzac tackles details of human character within his narratives, one realises what a brilliant writer he is. His characters are never more than representatives of the usual stereotypes we come across; rather, they are caricatures of the all-encompassing social and moral issues that perpetually haunt Paris. With his brilliant eye for detail, Balzac ensures that his characters are as believable as those one meets on the streets – a blend of good and evil, strong and weak. Among the techniques that I consider most admirable is the merging of the characters' physical features with their expressions, facial features, and even emotions. There is a similar grace and sophistication in the way the writer's portrayal of the subject's appearance, style of dressing, and general conduct discloses what is behind the mask. This is the technique that grants the reader the ability to not only see but to deeply feel and empathise with the characters.

Also, Balzac appears to have a psychological realism which enables him to explore the intricate minds of the characters he creates and depicts in his works. Through their self-reflective glances and inner dialogues, he exposes the multifaceted hopes and fears that lie concealed. This added dimension of psychology renders the characters believable and significantly deepens the narrative. Balzac's mastery over language use is one of his biggest strengths.

This analysis will concern itself with the intricate social hierarchies and power structures that Balzac created in Paris. These social structures are blended together within the dialogues, enabling us to analyse the characters, their lives, and their membership in the tableau, and critique the relations that emerge. Additionally, Balzac employs striking metaphors when describing the speech of his characters. Like all adept writers, he does so figuratively, as all greats do. Core settings, as well as a variety of other subjects and features that dominate the narrative, are expressly and metaphorically inscribed in the text as embodying the people's wishes, wants, and moral conflicts. These symbols serve as the foundation for the "imagery" which informs the reader of the characters and ideas within the book. Balzac struggled with the task of writing a profile of every character. However, he stores in his capable hands a thorough account of the everyday life of members of Parisian society. He renders these paradoxical characters into a vivid, complex representation of self-preservation, achievement, and despair. This shift toward post-structuralist escapism makes the world a truly captivating place to discover, and seek after great literature.

I believe that Paris should be thought of not as a destination, but rather a character, or even a light that illuminates the world. Balzac was very capable of intricately differentiating the details of Paris and that is precisely why he was able to portray Paris as a light of the world. The setting in which Balzac situated his stories, like the characters, were very integral to the plot. Paris and all other places experienced change and expansion during the first half of the 1800s, and Balzac was sure to capture these changes. Paris is especially important to the context of Balzac's narratives, who described it as his condition base. This greatly encouraged memorisation of the city. Thus, Paris became France, and particularly Balzac's in the centre of art, politics, education which were the focus of cultural activities and profoundly influenced the writer's creations. No writer was such a master of using the varied cultures in his writing like he was. Balzac's Paris illustrates the result of the uneven progress of an evolving civilisation.

The wealthy parts of the city are bounded by dirt-stained streets, showing a clear division of inequality and poverty. Paris is not only the epitome of beauty, but is also the inspiration of almost all components of creation and invention, as well as the depth of conflict and scope found in Balzac's work.

Balzac illustrates Paris in greater detail, not only as the setting of the tale, but also as an integral character that determines the life of the people in the story. He depicts the romantic dreams and the tragic despair and hope of people who Paris, more so than any other novel by Balzac, encapsulates.

It has to be noted, however, that structures such as Notre-Dame Cathedral as well as various joyful boulevards managed to earn their own symbolism within Balzac's texts. These structures did not serve purely physical functions. The socio-political phenomena that were occurring in Paris at the time sculptured Balzac as much as he sculpted them in his texts. Indeed, it is a rich context for the phenomenon of the complexity of human existence and the struggles it faces. Consequently, it will be essential to assess what these phenomena were in order to comprehend fully how Balzac pictured Paris. His celebrated works span from the depiction of powerful literary salons to the founding of new art schools, and those are the features that most admired Balzac because he did not leave the spirit of the epoch outside his narratives. This does not only capture the imagination of the audience, but most importantly pushes them to contemplate the problems and conflicts that the characters face.

Indeed, Balzac saw Paris not only as a collection of monuments but as a lively embodiment of his work - a city of perpetual motion. Balzac's Paris allows the reader to dive right into a civilisation that functions on the interplay of culture, history and social life that circulates around his characters. There are defining features that allow the readers to appreciate how his crafted literature has shaped the world.

Social Representations Analysis of Balzac

It can be stated without any doubt that Balzac's reception was somber and complex, and as such, there are several poems where he himself captures the social and psychological issues of the French. Balzac and society were united in Paris, and together they created a powerful 'yes' that, in rhythm with other fellows, emerged in the capital. He was both praised and condemned by the critics and later generations. As the words poured from his pen, zeal for his work was bestrewn on the readers and the critics for how effectively he managed to portray the futile efforts of his characters to rise above social constraints. Critics were polarised after the publication of 'La Comédie Humaine' as his high society portrayal of urban life was rather liberal than conservative. It was received well as one of the best works of urban literature, but the morality of the work was scorned. The untouched portrayal of man was equally stunning and terrifying.

Moreover, Balzac's frame of reference was bound to be distinct from that of readers today. In fact, every succeeding generation has a fresh approach towards art due to the changes brought about by culture with the passage of time. All readers from different corners of the world for different periods of time have been able to relate to him owing to the eloquent depiction of his characters who rose above social boundaries. Aspects of Balzac's social portrayal still remain a matter of debate among critics and academics in the 20th and 21st century. A considerable number concur that Balzac has profoundly impacted people and their culture in general. This is precisely the debate that Balzac's work poses regarding a writer's obligation towards the society they write about. Literature, and particularly the author's depiction of human nature and political might, as well as moral dilemmas, poses worrying questions about the social function of literature. Balzac's work has indeed provoked debate regarding the obligations placed on writers and the ethics and limitations of the representations they create, as well as the more controversial issue of whether fiction is appropriate to use for commenting on real events.

In general, both this society and this literature appear to handle the artist's creative liberties and moral responsibilities exceptionally well. In other words, the reception of Balzac's portrayal of society shows the enormous debate concerning the relations of his literary and social works.

This controversial topic has sparked a new conversation regarding the society - art relationship and the controversies which may be created in the mind. The numerous attacks made against Balzac have enhanced our understanding of the strength of his images of society. Without doubt, many readers and scholars of literature marvel at Balzac's works.

Accustoming the modern public: Understanding today's foreigners

Along with the jaws of a finely wrought wolf, a deep essence recalls him from Balzac's life and marks his metamorphoses, as wonderfully captured in Louis Remy's 1882 Imaginary Biography concerning a Parisian aesthetician illustrated as a person transitioning to a head snapped to a glitzy dreamlike path heading towards the finest society hoping to escape his poverty-stricken life. Facing this enormous quote from Balzac is very timely and indeed allows for broader context and deeper understanding. Because Balzac sketches the life of Parisian society in France during the 19th century, it gives other countries the need to do the same within their borders so that they would truly understand the psyche and soul of the country as a whole. Balzac passes across a collage of shifting nuances of the pain urban life can cause and the love and trust sown through betrayal and greed alongside the amazing perseverance which the human race possesses. Balzac, in his treatise, instead emphasises the so-called beauty of humanity's patterns over all other things.

Additionally, the range of personalities in Balzac's work is captivating from the perspective of contemporary audiences, with their varying motives and problems. The rich spectrum of social hierarchies encourages readers to contemplate values and choices and promotes empathy as well as moral development. At the same time, his analysis of social stratification, the difference between affluence and poverty, and the struggle for power by creative means is important in that it helps readers evaluate the social context in which they exist on a level that is utmost broad. Balzac's creations reveal the social structures of... representation for scrutiny with that emblematic of his brand of genius. More than a chronological period or a geo-culture, it appeals to the creative capacity of the analytical reader to extract and appreciate Balzac's systematic alterations. The fiction reader of Balzac is impelled to a cogitation upon class distinction, social mobility, and the capitalization of life.

In any case, the contemporary world is confronted with the dynamics of ethics, ambition, personal relations, and other complexities of one's existence, all of which are addressed by Balzac's works, bestowing upon us opportunities that shall never cease to be valued.

THE THEMES OF LE PÈRE GORIOT

Ambition and Corruption

An Overview of Le Père Goriot

With the publication of 'Le Père Goriot', Honoré de Balzac attains the height of his socio-historical achievement within the context of early nineteenth-century France, capturing in the work the social changes and desires of people during the time. France, much like the rest of the world, experienced a marked change in social and economic conditions subsequent to the Industrial Revolution, which brought with it a good deal of new wealth in contrast with the already existing social stratification.

It is within this context that Balzac set out to tackle a more controversial literary issue: the 'selfish' ambition-corruption-power triad. The audience of this novel is treated to a detailed depiction of Parisian society, dominated by the folly of self-advancement where ever-increasing wealth and status is the only goal worth pursuing, as morality and self-respect slowly become non-existent. Taking place during the post-Napoleonic period, 'Le Père Goriot' examines in detail how historical events affect individuals at a personal level. Balzac, through astute observation and deep empathy, unfurls a narrative that navigates the complexities of class structure, highlighting the growing chasm between the aristocracy and the rising middle class. The novel also depicts the corruption and ambition that fuel most people, which can be compared to the reality of politics, economy, and social relations.

At the heart of the story, 'Le Père Goriot' reveals the complexity of anthropological aspirations and the moral issues that stem from excessive ambition. Balzac's sensitivity to the human and sociocultural comprises the body of the work, as he explores the reasons behind a character's actions and decisions. The work highlights the social structures that propel ambition, revealing the hardships of people trying to climb up the social ladder in a decaying moral society. Balzac's sensitivity to the human and sociocultural comprises the body of the work, as he explores the reasons behind a character's actions and decisions. The work highlights the social structures that propel ambition, revealing the hardships of people trying to climb up the social ladder in a decaying moral society. 'Le Père Goriot' immerses readers in the vortex of nineteenth-century France, a perfect setup from which to analyse the multi-dimensional issues of ambition, greed, and the tendency to seek feigned importance in existence. Balzac does not only design the prose but also the history, which segues readers into pondering whether the themes are still relevant now.

The Nature of Ambition: Character Analysis

Over the course of the novel, 'Le Père Goriot', Balzac elaborates on the theme of ambition using deeply nuanced characters. The mental quest for power and subsequently class prestige is fully realised in the characters Rastignac, Vautrin, and Goriot himself.

With dreams of joining high society, Rastignac, a law student from the provinces, is enchanted by the glamour that Paris has to offer. Though he navigates his morality while chasing success, he is the living proof of boundless ambition. Vautrin, on the other hand, is the alter ego of Rastignac. He elicits ambition of a darker realm where he employs manipulation and lies in order to dominate his adversaries. Additionally, Vautrin is a brilliant planner to the degree that he depicts self-interested ambition that wants to overpower the world. On a different spectrum, we have Goriot who, in the name of ambition, portrays a parent who loves his daughters unconditionally and seeks validation through their achievements. In this manner, through these clashing characters, Balzac offers a deep insight into the multifaceted nature of ambition, along with its perks, problems, and influence on society and its people.

These different pursuits of ambition by society create hunger which serves as a reflection of the covets of that society. Readers are drawn into the varied levels of ambition of each character to confront the reality of the world and how it is driven by recognition. Thus, Balzac, in detail and profoundly, presents a society's desire to reflect on the dark side of society and the reasons behind desire and the fallout of pursuing those ambitions. In-depth self-reflection leads to a rich story that attracts the audience's attention as well as makes them reflect on what ambition is within works of fiction and real life.

Social Climbing and Its Costs

In Le Père Goriot, Balzac thoroughly analyses the social issue of social climbing and goes as far as documenting its wide-ranging effects. The novel offers a rich tapestry of characters whose lust for social advancement is so great that they are willing to pay any price to achieve it. Balzac goes beyond basic character sketching and carefully explains what drives them to seek more power and prestige. More than that, he wantonly shows how weak both the family and the economy can be if the only guiding impetus is ambition, exposing the myth of social advancement. Balzac maintains elegance while exercising his observational acumen in his writings, balancing the exposition with the explanation of the ills that underlie the very power and wealth one strives to attain, resulting in corruption. The sharp transition from Goriot, Rastignac, and Vautrin depicting Parisian society to the focus being on the even darker side serves as a lesson; a lesson hiding a price to be paid for ever-increasing ambitions and upward growth.

The sharp transition from Goriot, Rastignac, and Vautrin depicting Parisian society to the focus on the even darker side serves as a lesson; a lesson hiding a price to be paid for ever-increasing ambitions and upward growth.

The perils of social climbing are captured as the story evolves, suggesting the ensuing moral collapse and psychological disintegration one has to deal with as a result of such pursuits. These dynamics depict not just the Parisian society in the nineteenth century, but even more so present-day society, which invites the readers to ponder upon the consequences of ambition on self and society. Balzac's keen eye on social stratifications and the consequences of them over Balzac's Goriot makes it much more than a narrative story; it transforms it into a deeply moving commentary on humanity and ambition's place in society.

Crisis in the Economic and Familial Relationship

In Le Père Goriot, Honoré de Balzac writes plain fiction that touches the subtle yet intricate details of corruption based on family and economic structures. He shows Goriot, Rastignac, and Vautrin as characters whom Balzac portrays so effortlessly that one can easily see the moral weakness that exists among these individuals. The economic corruption is set in Parisian society and is depicted through manipulation, exploitation, and greed that seems to weave through the entire society. It portrays the moral depravity that one develops in the chase for wealth and power and the devastating effect that such things have on family and one's own self.

The imbalance of economic activities and familial relations catalyses the extremely unethical practice of chicanery and the moral decay of society as we know it today. In addition to this, it also provides a powerful contrast to the examination of Parisian corruption with its ostentatious grandeur while serving as a backdrop for Balzac's portrayal of the squalid underbelly of societal mechanisms. He captures Paris as a city of progression, which unfortunately comes at the enormous cost of society's foundational principles. This causes people to step over those principles and treacherously abandon them to get ahead. This, in turn, highlights the extreme and uncontrolled ambition that the bourgeois possess. This disintegration of values is further exacerbated by the intertwining intricacies of family and economic corruption. Such a blend culminates in the compromise of personal ambition with systemic deficiencies. Balzac further depicts the lack of moral foundation of the family's power, the unit, with the theme of corruption. The power struggle within the family reflects Balzac's fear of dominance and what it entails in society as a whole. The portrayal of highly acute observations is extremely corrupt in nature, adversely affecting all layers of society while also dating deep within the familial bond; Balzac captures all these elements. On the other hand, as characters get deeper and deeper into the cynical and overbearing struggle for dominance, their paths become more treacherous and the bond of family more corrupt, completely severing the last strands of moral foundation they had left. All this together causes existential desolation within themselves.

Balzac doesn't just tell us about the exploitation of economic and family structures; he also vividly depicts the tragic neglect of morals in society, including how it exists today. Similarly, Balzac's 'Le Père Goriot' is an insightful work on how the lack of ethics in society destroys the values people hold dear in history. He achieved this through detailed development of literary characters and telling us how people descended deeper into the darkness in the chase for money and social standing.

The Role of Paris in Fostering Ambition

Like in many cases, Paris, the city of romance and lights, is not different when it comes to these concepts; it is at the same time a beautiful canvas and the focus of attention for many people. From Balzac's perspective on Provence, Paris represents both danger and opportunity. In 'Le Père Goriot', the reader can almost feel the city's rich flavour; Paris in particular demonstrates the opposing view that there is great opportunity out there that one must make use of. It is no secret that the streets of Paris are filled with people today wishing to make something of themselves, and in turn gives rise to many lofty dreams. People who look forward to 'making it' do not see the entrapments of desire, influences of wealth, and status that accompany this pursuit, and instead view the beautiful city as a free paradise.

The focus shows Paris as an amalgamation of rich and poor because the pavements continue from the lavish parlours of aristocrats to some dark slums. Geographically, each area more clearly builds upon the notion of ambition, becoming a stage where characters battle with the duality of themselves and their plans, each more intricate than the other. Additionally, the delicate historic and cultural structure of Paris paints the city as a paranormal place with a rich variety of nuances, where ambition is the core theme. Alongside the breathtaking architecture and history, the characters of the city's ambitions become steeped in the ozone as they participate in the unending waltz with the ghosts of unsolved mysteries of the past and the almost promised future. Paris serves as a glamorous painting, but a vicious one at that. Balzac paints Paris as a seductive sculptress with no mercy, for the city forges the hopes and moral principles of the people living there.

Paris serves as a glamorous painting, but a vicious one at that. Balzac paints Paris as a seductive sculptress with no mercy, for the city forges the hopes and moral principles of the people living there. From yet another point of view, Paris is a stark gold place, a place with potential, a place that serves as a trigger for inward searching, forcing characters to confront the inner chaos created due to the hunger for ambition. Paris encourages self-criticism and ethical issues, helping characters find their way.

Indeed, Balzac describes Paris as containing a Montesquieuan aura that transfigures every being to succumb to the empire of ambition whilst simultaneously diverging from the perpetrators of it. As power is so strongly pursued in Le Père Goriot by the rest, it serves as a potent weapon to serve Balzac's pedagogical response to Aviary. Through the competition between Parisian opulence and depravity, he decisively highlights the fundamental impact the city relation has with the hopes of his characters. The degree of invention and the depth of vice is rarely matched anywhere else in the world.

In Le Père Goriot, Gaston perfectly embodies the idea of the pursuit of power within the fabric of 19th-century Parisian society. He is single-mindedly driven and willing to go to any lengths to achieve his ambitions. This is an accurate portrayal of the consequences that overreaching ambition can have on a person. With impeccable scholarship, the author weaves themes of cunning intelligence with determination to reveal the complex web of Parisian society. His preoccupations with strength and authority are personal, political, and economic all at once. This exemplifies Balzac's concern with the darker aspects of human psychology. The dominance-seeking Gaston is an eternal testimony to the ethical rot and deviation that occurs in a society that is openly competitive and lacks a moral framework. Furthermore, through the lens of a single character, Balzac attempts to generalise Gaston's character to demonstrate the moral compulsions that exist in society and the tendencies to resolve these, leading to the ready transformation of a power seeker. Balzac's vision of Paris is very idealistic and, in particular, harsh towards the continuous existence of this social structure. He explains it using Goriot as the source of information about the processes that lead to society's deep corruption.

Symbolism of Wealth and Moral Decay

In 'Le Père Goriot,' Balzac portrays the correlation between wealth and moral decay within Parisian society, using wealth as a plush metaphor. The luxurious possessions, including the beautiful apartments, doors, and salons, reflect the inner decay and immoral rot of the characters. The details of the imagined lifestyle, alongside the dark desires of society's ambition, irresistibly imbalance morality and reveal the beauty in Balzac's writing.

The theme of moral decay is further elaborated in the characterisation of Vautrin, a shrewd and unscrupulous figure in the novel, who personifies a ruthless, morally bankrupt capitalist. His refined manipulations and utter contempt for accepted norms demonstrate the level of moral and ethical depravity that could be inflicted upon a civilisation where immense social value is placed on personal wealth, exceeding any form of personal virtue. Furthermore, Balzac pays special attention to the setting by embedding faint and crude symbols of decay, such as dilapidated buildings, dirty streets, and impoverished areas, depicting the metaphorical loss of values and the harmful nature of ambition without limits. These images and symbols serve as a warning against the severe consequences of materialism gone awry, with the alteration of social strata as the goal. The contradiction of wealth and moral decay is evident even in the glaring paradox of the glittering life of the upper class and the mundane existence of the poorer side of the prosperous world.

The overarching theme of wealth's imagery and its moral decay, as depicted in 'Le Père Goriot', serves as a raw representation of the negative effects of ambition and materialism on individual esteem and societal unity. Balzac employs metaphors and imagery, coupled with the discussion of these themes, in a way that resonates with readers as timeless, forcefully making one reflect on the darker sides of human nature and the dire consequences of the untamed thirst for wealth and prestige.

Interpersonal Relationships: A Study of Influence

One of the central themes of Balzac's Le Père Goriot is the gripping, undiscovered world of relationships, both social and professional, and their insatiable impact on individual ambitions and morals. More accurately, power, wealth, and social status—yearned for by the characters—are commensurate with their interactions with other members of society. This reveals the complexities of human behaviour and the structure of society. By examining these relationships, we appreciate the motivations behind the characters and the intricacies of the plot while critiquing corruption and ambition. Vautrin's and Eugène de Rastignac's relationship is perhaps one of the most complex in the book.

As Rastignac roams through Paris's class-conscious society in pursuit of social mobility, Vautrin serves both as a guide and a schemer, revealing the fine line between friendship and opportunism. This duality demonstrates the beauty and weaknesses of ambition while illustrating the importance that one's relationships have on their desires and moral constraints. Likewise, the crossroads of their lives allow for insight into how Balzac depicts the damaging aspects of the societal ecosystem by distinguishing between ambition and ethical deterioration. In addition, Goriot's relationship with his daughters, especially with Anastasie and Delphine, raises sensitive issues concerning family relations and personal ambition. His love and care for his daughters starkly contrast with their love for money and their father's name. Balzac expertly balances the conflicts and weaknesses within these relationships, illustrating the struggles of the family with desires and the erosion of ethics under the authority of ambition. This characterisation sheds light on the wider theme of ambition and bribery while showcasing the overpowering nature of relationships in the characters' life decisions.

The cross-level relationships between characters express the correlation of social classes, providing a multidimensional analysis of power and control. Balzac was able to capture the spells cast by power, suggesting cunningness masked by social settings ranging from self-serving aristocracy to grasping, self-serving social climbers. The seemingly civilised moves that Balzac sought to weave into the dialogues and gestures are laced with the overpowering threads that shape the characters' wills and deeds, revealing the binding interdependence of social relations and the pursuit of desire. Power may take different forms; it may be latent or exercised openly. All these forms of power relationships foster multilevel agendas and serve the need for self-serving goals.

The study of relationships in Le Père Goriot illustrates the intertwining nature of ambition and moral evil, revealing the multifaceted nature of sociological paradigms. These power dynamics lead to Balzac's salutary depiction of layers integrated into the story, inviting readers to contemplate the enduring concern of social relations in relation to inner desires and the ethical dilemmas rooted in them.

Literary Techniques to Depict Ambition

Le Père Goriot is a representation of how Balzac employed multiple literary devices to demonstrate the corrosive nature of overwhelming ambition. The very structure of the narrative reveals Balzac's deep understanding of humanity and society through the unique lens of characterisation. One of the most prominent representations of healthy ambition is Eugène de Rastignac. His life is filled with experiences that readers may both envy and fear. Balzac captures Rastignac's inner conflict and moral dilemmas in detail, illustrating his deep ambition and the reasoned decisions that follow. Additionally, the author examines ambition through imagery, focusing on its insatiable nature. He employs a technique in which he describes a gaping hole of moral ethic, which contributes to society's further descent into the wealth of the world, where distortion appears alongside poverty. Furthermore, Balzac uses narrative technique to depict the growth of ambition and its effects on a character's life. The slow, inevitable growth of a character towards the negative aspects of ambition is encapsulated remarkably well through the transformations of Goriot and Rastignac.

Sacrifice, betrayal, and self-serving themes define this change, which, through Balzac's powerful storytelling, immerses the reader in a deep sea of moral fog. Communication between characters, delivered in an unrivalled manner, brings new life to the novel, allowing readers to navigate the ever-tense world of aspiration. Balzac masterfully depicts the nuance of ambition and how it weaves itself through interpersonal relationships, while also exposing the collateral damage it can cause through foreshadowing and dramatic irony. Unchecked ambition can lead to destructive outcomes, and Balzac reminds readers of the realities of societal values versus personal ambition. He not only seeks to inform but also challenges readers with profound introspection. Literature serves as a tool to elucidate the disturbing and serene nature of unchecked ambition, and this is why Balzac compels readers to reconsider their own preconceived notions on the subject.

In conclusion, the societal critique presented in the novel suggests that ambition and corruption serve as fascinating themes for exploration. The literary techniques intertwine the various strands of power, ambition, and moral degradation within both the fictional characters and Parisian society. Like other novels, this one too illustrates how unchecked ambition results in dire and unfortunate consequences, shedding light on the darker side of humanity.

Moreover, the representation of social standing and reputation in the novel and their consequences offers a compelling critique of how status and wealth constantly influence human actions. Balzac's emphasis on the disorder in the economic and familial systems points out the divided directions in which personal aspirations and ethical considerations pull, compelling readers to grapple with the nuances of human motivation versus social pressure. Paris is the significant context, as it plays an integral role in ambition and corruption. It is both the source and the outcome of how characters relentlessly pursue dominance, with its busy streets and luxurious salons serving as a metaphor for the endless quest for recognition. Balzac perfectly balances the tension between the urban environment and the ambitions of the characters, enhancing the sociological criticism of the book. Gaston's sober image arises from this fatal desire for power and riches, vividly depicting the perils of excessive ambition, particularly the moral decay and personal losses that typically accompany it. The imageries of wealth and moral corruption intersect, revealing strong concerns regarding the absence of values and principles in the ceaseless struggle for economic success.

The brutality of human ambitions, as captured by Balzac, can be observed as he explains relationships and how they influence individuals. The relationships between characters in the novel are crafted to explain societal corruption and how ambition manifests itself within society. This book, like all of Balzac's works, remains a timeless masterpiece that reflects and critiques the conflict between desires and morality. In Le Père Goriot, the author captures the intricate web of the human psyche, allowing the reader to reflect on the darker side of one's desires. Corruption and the pursuit of ambition remain the enduring themes of all civilisations, and Balzac encapsulates these truths in every sentence of the book.

LOVE, LOSS, AND LITERARY REALISM

The Romantic Ideals in Balzac's Works

In the work of Honoré de Balzac, there is always a contradiction between the romantic ideal and the motives behind the character's actions. In the series of novels known as La Comédie Humaine, love, passion, and idealism are expertly woven alongside the reality of existence by Balzac. His characters serve as a prologue to intimate chronicles that study the conflicting facets of emotions and human desires. In contrast to many romantic writers, Balzac did not restrict himself to pure objectivity. Instead, he intricately delved into the notions of the human psyche. He tackles love and passion with utmost skill and adds layers of emotion and detail to his narratives. The way Balzac incorporates romantic ideals in his works of art shows that a man can examine the human essence with all its intricacies whenever he wants to understand love. His characters, motivated quite diversely, turn passionately in love, seeking to satisfy their aims and find themselves within the illusions created by life that often result in pain and despair. Romance for Balzac is not purely about love. Rather, his understanding of romantic ideals is far removed from the conventional approach and deeply rooted in the emotions, aspirations, and societal constructs within human relationships.

Balzac's multifaceted storytelling strategy resonates powerfully with his readers, providing them with a deep understanding of the world. The romantic elements in Balzac's works are central to the enigmas of human feelings and their goals, leading to works that are not merely sentimental, but that evoke a fuller comprehension of human nature. These themes are not confined to a specific time or culture, but rather speak to the universal human experience, making the audience feel included and understood.

Expositions Of Backbreaking Sorrow: The Truths Of Affection And Reality

One of the most painful aspects of love in Balzac's works is the raw depiction of the messy and bittersweet realities of romance. Heartbreak and its disappointments are part of the realities of Balzac's characters. The author gives insight into the emotional depths of people through the eyes of his characters in an untouched and often quite disturbing way. Because of Balzac's sensitivity to the human spirit, he can reproduce the pain of unreturned love, the loss of love, and the aching anguish of gaps and the effects of loss. Such loss and pain are neither exaggerated nor playful in any way but represent a chilling view of the harshness of life and love. This raw and relatable portrayal of human emotions in Balzac's characters fosters a sense of connection and empathy in the audience.

By virtue of the intricacies of his narrative style, Balzac dazzles the readers with the intimate type of heartache and how it impacts the universe as a whole. The emotional chaos his characters undergo replicates the genuine strife of the people in society. As readers, we find ourselves fascinated by oppression, the loss of dreams, and disappointment, clearly visible in Balzac's works. As the loss of love or heartbreak for Balzac is not regarded as something trivial but rather an underlying theme within the fabric balanced through human experience, it serves as a painful reminder of how profound love can be and how deep the scars it leaves behind can be. Through the powerful means of storytelling, he constructs a framework within which the readers can understand all parts of the world. Hence, in his works, Balzac engrosses and captivates his audience through the unification of heartbreak. This theme transcends time and culture. Ultimately, Balzac's profound depiction of heartbreak and how it impacts life and love draws the reader in and captivates them through the power of literary art. It also serves as a reminder to the reader of human nature's harsh yet undiluted truths.

Comparing Eros with Ambition

The collection of motives surrounding love and ambition has always been intriguing and appealing in the literary arena.

Honoré de Balzac, a profound analyst, skillfully intertwines love and ambition in his writing. Characters in pursuit of love are no different from those striving for professional success. Balzac's keen observation of the desire for power, wealth, and social acceptance, and the passion of love, provides a deep, meaningful distinction between the two. This analogy sheds light on the broader spectrum of human existence, revealing their deepest desires and the lengths they are willing to go to fulfil them.

Furthermore, Balzac identifies these parallel aspects in pairing the societal situation in his timeframe with the one today. The bondage between the passion for love and the ambition towards achievement may offer victory but also lead to tragedy. Balzac captures this quite masterfully in his fiction through his character-building. One of the most remarkable aspects of this comparison is the revelation of the influence of personal relationships on characters' aspirations.

In Balzac's works, the stark relationship between unfulfilled and passionate desires is an important driving force for the characters. It enables them to tackle ambition and strive for social and economic values. From this perspective, the thematic content of Balzac deepens tremendously. It also provides an opportunity for the readers to reflect upon similar themes present in their lives. The interplay of love and ambition, believed by Balzac, provides insight into the complex branches of human motivation, shedding light on the eternal struggle to achieve satisfaction by any means, including affection, love, or success.

Character Study: Idealists and Their Tragic Love

Balzac's examination of tragic lovers and ideal thinkers rang through his words. Romance is boldly depicted in the works of Balzac's characters. The Balzac characters reveal the intricacies of emotions and the frailties of humanity. Balzac, through realism, depicts the internal conflict and the intricacies caused by the love and dreams of the characters. It is crucial to realise that the tragic destinies of his characters are not only structural devices for telling a story but rather testimony to the sad realities of life where dreams are constantly shattered.

Thanks to the nuances offered in Balzac's character development, readers can relate to these individuals not only at a personal level but also concerning the challenges posed by society, making the plight of these characters incredibly heartbreaking and moving. The unreported adoration of Eugène de Rastignac in 'Le Père Goriot' to the active neo-romantic fantasies of Lucien de Rubempré in 'Illusions Perdues' is brilliantly handled by Balzac, which reveals the tormented idealism that is core to 'love'. In addition, Balzac captures the intricacies of human ambition and the psychological evaluation of his characters, where he endows them with moral responsibility and blunders, offering restive judgement from the Bolshevik ideology of self-sacrifice. Balzac's blend of lucidity and profundity allows the reader to contemplate the spelling issues of love and the magical dream of accomplishment and even happiness. The masterfully crafted Balzac portrays the internal aspects of tragic love through his enigmatic narratives, giving clues and suggestions without avowing directly, enabling myriad generations and cultures to find solace in the depths of his knowledge and love for humanity, proving that the intelligence regarding the human heart never changes.

Balzac's Stylistic Techniques for Emotional Depth

French novelist Honoré de Balzac uses several stylistic techniques to give breath and gain to the emotions incorporated into and around his character.

In this, Balzac's artistry shines through in the ability to blend poignance within emotion and human relations concerning its psychological and sentimental dimensions. Perhaps Balzac's techniques are best displayed through the detailed and nuanced descriptions of the physical environment and how he balances them with the characters' psychological state. Balzac intricately outlines the setting and depicts the characters as deeply disturbed. As a result, the facets of their surroundings become emblems of their mental state. Other than fostering a world where the reader can imagine the settings, such a technique depicts the narrative's emotional turbulence.

Additionally, this method offers deeper meaning and imagery, functioning as a metaphor for the intricacies of the characters' emotions. Another technique employed by Balzac, through his use of admirable introspective monologue and internal dialogues, further balances the readers' depth of understanding between the setting and the character. His works are so skilled in portraying emotions that readers can profoundly understand the character's feelings. Doing so, however, invites one deeper into the character's psyche, which is Balzac's intent, which further affirms his lead in the pursuit of understanding emotions.

The use of specific and recurring themes and symbols not only gives Balzac's prose a pleasing poetic quality but also enforces the emotional aspect of a story. Balzac employs specific colours, the meaning behind particular objects, and the nature around a scene to highlight the emotions behind the tale and add rich symbolic meaning. Additionally, Balzac's effective construction of dialogue adds to the overall emotional appeal of his works. Their conversations do not occur in a void but are rather laced with unexpressed feelings and tension. This further complicates the relationships between the characters. Dialogues offer insights into the characters' feelings and imply their happiness, sadness, hopes, and frustrations.

In conclusion, one may marvel at Balzac's stylistic mastery of infusing deep emotions into an account of profound significance to the genre of literary realism. Balzac is a true skilled wizard in details, uses rich language, and deeply grasps human emotions. This sets him apart as unique, ensures his literary work transcends all of time, and is a source of inspiration to countless readers and writers.

Critique of the use of Sentimentality in Literature

The concept of sentimentality in literature has been under scrutiny and criticism for quite a long time by people in literature. This is a thin line that many writers like Honoré de Balzac treaded on carefully, not wanting to slip into deep emotional expressions. Sentiments have the potential to stir emotions in the readers. Still, in excessive amounts, they could gravely be a disservice to the entire story. Balzac, known for the illustrious ways he captured the inner workings of man's emotions, was admirably judicious in his use of sentiment in a way that brought through understanding and not overcluttered drama. Instead of sticking exclusively to romanticism, Balzac aimed for the more complex core of human feeling and emotional expression. He used his keen perception and ability in psychological analysis to achieve a lasting, well-rounded feeling. The assessment of sentimentality within a work of literature confirms the essential need to understand the context and the viewer's sensitivity. When applied in moderation, sentimental motives portray characters and plots more realistically. Too often, a good thing, however, risks making the more nuanced portrayal of feelings irrelevant to the work's effectiveness. The criticism of Balzac toward the excessive use of sentimentality tells us of one powerful thing: sincere emotions can be expressed through smart social issues. Cling to the notion that people are not overly sentimental.

By focusing on the ordinary and the routine, Balzac turned into a master of literary realism, leaving behind an everlasting mark on the world. The criticism of sentimentality in literature begs for contemplation of the very fine line separating neural feeling from sham dramatics and calls for a deeper understanding of human beings, minus sham emotionalism, from writers.

Loss As Means Of Character Building

In fiction, loss is one of the most powerful means of character building, enabling authors to examine the extremes of human emotion and strength. The diverse experiences of loss, including grief, heartache, letdown and failure, can all be found in the crafted works of Honoré de Balzac. In La Comédie Humaine, readers get introduced to various characters who suffer severe personal losses and/or setbacks, whether material, emotional, or relational. And for the readers, all of these factors enable the characters to evolve throughout the narrative. Balzac eloquently explores how people experience and deal with loss in one of the many aspects, where he depicts an individual's transformation and/or changes in a societal context. Balzac's exploration of the various effects of loss shows the potential of not only tearing apart a person's identity but also the mere change Balzac suggests is needed for an individual to achieve an alteration that is felt within the character and society.

In addition, the writer skillfully shows the effect of loss and how it can change a person on a fundamental level, as well as the self-reflection that follows this loss, which increases the depth of his character. With Balzac's adept use of characterisation and psychological insight, he shows how his protagonists overcome their hardships, viewing loss as an opportunity to rediscover and enlighten themselves. Balzac's characters shed their personas forged through life struggles. Through the alchemical loss process, they are reborn with a deeper understanding of self. On a greater scale, the relationship between loss and society exposes the personal experiences about the society's spirit. Balzac is masterful in depicting the nuances of their loss and how individual tragedy and upheaval within relationships tend to question social norms, reveal weakness, and reorder relations. His readers must ponder personal suffering and how it contributes to overall cultural change. His readers must ponder personal suffering and how it contributes to cultural change. Through the adept demonstration of the numerous ways in which loss overly affects the trajectory of his characters, Balzac illustrates the important lesson of how self-discovery is crucial after facing adversity.

The Effect of Relationships on Society as a Whole

In Balzac's novels, personal relationships are much more complex than simple love affairs. They provide a profound commentary about society. His characterisations and observations allow him to offer a vivid picture of interlinked lives on a canvas where Balzac places many actions beyond a single person and affect an entire society. Balzac provides an insight into marriages, friendships and even family relations that tend to inform changes in values, power, and behaviour across society. He shows that in any given community, people are deeply interconnected and are influenced by one another in complex manners. There is no doubt that personal relationships have a bearing on society. Balzac's insights have a bearing on personal relationships outside the family context. His narratives shed light on the direct consequences of such relationships on economy, politics, culture and everything in between. The nuances of love, desire, and social mobility Balzac addresses exemplify how deeply rooted the effects an individual has on society.

This thematic treatment deepens the emotional engagement of Balzac's works. It simultaneously animates the social and historical context in which his story is situated. Balzac uses personal relationships to reveal how tradition is sustained and altered or turned on its head. He depicts characters' complex relationships in their worlds, i.e., he shows the importance of personal relations in shaping and changing societal attitudes. Therefore, Balzac's interpretation of personal relations is a peripheral look into the change in society as it illustrates the constant consequences of human relationships on the social fabric, which is perpetually altered.

La Comedie Humaine: A Gallery of Romantic Entanglements

Invoking a plethora of human feelings and relationships, Balzac, in his chief work, La Comedie Humaine, presents an enchanting gallery that goes beyond the very definition of love: romance. Romance in Balzac was and remains complicated, and at the heart of his graphic paintings is an even more profound appreciation of the intricacy of romantic relationships and the social effects they cause. The reader meets many characters, each involved in various romantic interests, and is thus confronted with the wide spectrum of human emotions - from burning desire to bone-chill dissatisfaction.

Balzac's careful study of romance enables him to craft a unique portrait of love that appeals to readers of any age. This theme is also visible in La Comedie Humaine, where Balzac's worldview enables us to enter the realities of love in its complexity and collectiveness, whether it is the Sedan frame or middle-class amalgamations. Each example of romance embodies human passion, aspiration, and the impact of a social structure. Furthermore, the interrelationships within and outside society narrate a fascinating story of emotions and actions filled with love and its consequences. As readers fully immerse themselves in the longing romances of the novel, they receive a dose of reflection that has always been relevant: love and all its emotions. As such, Balzac offers insightful anticipations on the interrelationships and romance without limitation to drama. It is particularly interesting how he explores the causes and effects of these complications. His characters, though presented in striking psychological detail, face the dilemmas of love and often find themselves battling with how to fulfil their ambitions versus the desires of society.

Such tensions give deep emotional context to the romantic stories and serve as a framework that allows Balzac to critique the cultural and societal expectations that his society placed during his time. In addition, while seeking out extreme romantic situations, Balzac reveals that love has its triumphs and tragedies for everyone in similar ways. Whether one looks at it temporally or spatially, human desire is always accompanied by all the struggles there are in the world, forever moulding and remoulding the fates of people and civilisations. In these complexities, Balzac captures the spirit of romanticism in the human condition and gives La Comédie Humaine a touch of timelessness.

Final Thoughts: The Personal Aspects in Balance With the Literary Artistry

The striking balance of personal emotions with literature in the work of Balzac leaves one wondering deeply about humanity. Balzac in La Comédie uses a great combination of realism and romanticism to express humanity's emotions- particularly love and its suffering.

This was unique in merging personal feelings and literature as it enables readers to explore the deepest parts of their being while experiencing the art of storytelling in its truest form, which is multifaceted. As Balzac paints the intricate details of interpersonal relationships, he accurately showcases the raw and powerful feelings that speak to readers of all ages, which speaks to the never-ending relevance of his works. Every character's passage of romance and heartbreak is a moving metaphor for the pain and elation that characterise humanity. Equally, Balzac's mastery of pen enables him to blend literature with emotions; readers coming across his work gain the appetite to open up to themselves, which fosters a deeper relationship between the characters and the reader. Balzac's writings' union of personal feelings and crafting encourages readers to embrace their emotions and become more self-aware, acting as a catalyst for compassion. This conjunction illustrates how relevant and important the portrayal of experiences through stories is. Balzac's works truly speak the languages of individual moments and the universal understanding of people.

In essence, Balzac never ceases to evoke interest and sympathy for readers, as we seem to write from an emotional inner core that is intricately woven with literary creativity. In other words, the blend of personal feelings and artistic imagination in Balzac's work leaves room for further reflection and harmony.

BALZAC'S EXPLORATION OF SOCIAL HIERARCHIES

Social Stratification in Balzac's World

To grasp the complexities of social stratification found in the works of Honoré de Balzac, it is essential to analyse the social structure of the early 19th century, which underwent drastic socio-economic changes. In the period in which Balzac lived in France, the country was experiencing a lot of transformations, including the consequences of the French Revolution and the onset of industrialisation. The aftereffects of the Revolution produced a Society that fought over equality and freedom while still deeply rooted in an established class system. Within this context, Balzac constructed his narratives to capture the shifting realities of social hierarchies. There arose a capitalist bourgeoisie who tried to consolidate their sociopolitical power as the noble class surrendered to their nostalgia for former glory. Balzac magnified these power relations and drew upon his perception of societal stratification in these novels. He gave readers and Society vivid imagery of the struggle between social traditions and modernity.

Balzac's works serve as a unique lens through which we can view the effects of social stratification on the society of his time. They provide a profound understanding of the socio-economic realities that deeply influence individual livelihoods. The stark gap between wealth and socioeconomic status, and the resulting activities, help explain the deeply resonant characters and the captivating plots that emerge in his works.

The Pursuit of Power by The Bourgeoisie

The structure of Balzac's world is filled with opposing elements, blended in such a way that the middle class culminates into a concrete force. Here, we will focus on their relentless pursuit of power and position and their never-ending struggle for recognition and social mobility. The bourgeoisie, as presented by Balzac, who lived through that era, represents the aggressive emergence of the middle class. A crucial detail Balzac provides in his accounts of the ambitions of the bourgeoisie is the details surrounding their background and overarching desire to not only better their status but significantly transform their position in society at large. This struggle for recognition and social mobility is a deeply human experience that Balzac's portrayal evokes in the audience.

Using Eugène de Rastignac in 'Le Père Goriot' or Lucien de Rubempré in 'Illusions perdues' provides insight into why and how the bourgeoisie set strategies to succeed and some moral and ethical compromises they faced. Balzac's depiction of these moral and ethical dilemmas faced by the bourgeoisie forces the audience to confront the complexities of social climbing and the costs it entails. Additionally, the interaction between the bourgeois characters and the aristocracy allows for exploring Balzac's world's social order and intricacies. Within these webs, a bourgeois head is an exclusive circle of societal influence, so attaining cultural capital is essential. The themes of Balzac's depiction of the bourgeoisie can be summed up in the most striking phrases: human capabilities, endurance, and the neverending thirst for authority. Through their highs and lows, Balzac forces his audience to think about the intricacies surrounding social climbing and what it means and costs. This exploration proves Balzac's understanding of the impressive nuances within the capture of the bourgeoisie's power-seeking motives. It gives the reader an insight into modern-day reflections on humanity.

The Role of the Clergy: Power, Influence, and Morality

Following Balzac, it is evident that the unrest in post-revolutionary France caused immense problems for the aristocracy, and the ability to adapt to new societal structures was vital for survival.

Balzac exhibits deep comprehension and skilful character structuring that concede readers an insightful view into the life of the noble class, which struggles with the loss of power and changing social structures.

In Balzac's fiction, the church is important not just because of its function but also for its cultural and political importance.

When looking at France in the nineteenth century, the church was mighty and often cut across the lines of the nobility and the bourgeoisie. Balzac accurately depicts the role of the church and clergy by analysing their moral responsibility, political activity, and social mobility. He features characters like the mysterious Abbé Herrera in “Lost Illusions” and the good-natured Félix de Vandenesse in “Memoirs of Two Young Wives,” who portray the profoundly different aspects of the clergy’s social role, as in the case of ambitious Abbé Carlos Herrera, who openly claimed the right to rule ‘the’ people, the church's independence from government restrictions created an unprecedented political power. As a historian, Balzac also serves to illuminate members of the clergy's self-inflicted moral plight from their internal hostilities in the face of great power.

Through an analysis of the complex relationships between the church and other social strata, Balzac incisively reveals the intricate structure of French society during the period. In addition, the church's lively interactions with the members of the nobility, the bourgeoisie, and the up-and-coming capitalist class add considerable depth to the thematic concerns of Balzac's works. The distinction between the pious and simple clergy, such as Félix de Vandenesse and the clerical intriguer and ambitious social climber Herrera, vividly captures the essence of the contrasting definitions of religious power. Furthermore, we see Balzac intensifying the sociopolitical issues by integrating moral aspects regarding the clergy, thus accentuating the unresolved tension between a moving idealism and a self-serving social reality. The religious leaders are, therefore, depicted as representing societal problems at a smaller scale, illustrating the complicated balance of power ethics and authority in the broader sense. Balzac's portrayal of these societal problems represented by the clergy makes the audience feel the weight of these issues and their impact on the society of his time.

The Impact of Industrialisation and The Growth of Capitalists

Industrialisation, along with the aftermath of World War II, was a pivotal factor that significantly altered the economic conditions of Balzac's era. The transition from traditional agricultural societies to urban centres brought about the emergence of a new class of capitalists with substantial financial power.

As traditional agricultural societies transitioned to urban centres, a new class of capitalists emerged with great financial power. The Industrial Revolution spurred industries like textiles, manufacturing, and transportation, leading to a concentrated wealth accumulation. Balzac became interested in how society changed as capitalists rose within the social strata, fighting the status quo and changing the balance of power. The rising capitalist class did not just accumulate tremendous wealth; they also attempted to gain dominance over political and cultural domains. With strong business acumen and savvy marriages, these people entered the sphere of politics. They made the lines between economic interests and morality almost indistinguishable. In Balzac's Europe, the rise of capitalists has always been a double-edged sword: bringing progress and growth for a few and obliteration and plunder for many. The power that capitalists wielded changed societal expectations and morality. To be materially successful was to hold social prestige, which meant a never-ending chase for wealth and power while sacrificing virtue.

Balzac explored the psychological workings of this development through the inner struggles and ethical conflicts of both the nouveaux riches and those trying to cope with a society of new inequalities. The clash between old aristocratic habits and the new capitalist society can be viewed as a rich source of Balzac's biting commentary on humanity and society's progression. Furthermore, the effect of industrialisation and the growing capitalism reverberated in the personal realm. It transformed the nature of love, marriage, and family. Balzac's characters confronted the consequences of socio-economic gaps and social mobility, in which love and marriage of convenience are contested. The family struggles in the face of conflicting aspirations. Balzac adeptly chronicled the complexities of love and loyalty and the need for financial prudence during fast-changing societies, carefully constructing characters and plots. While Balzac did not shy away from portraying the rise of capitalism in the years of the Industrial Revolution, he did so with great complexity, making him a great sociologist, as every detail of his work made him indulge in great speculation about humanity, morals, and disorder. His stories act as poignant and contemporary testimonies that dissect the effects of economic advancement and the social order, revealing yet another problematic impact of human ambition alongside morality.

The Effects of Class Structures on Individual Relationships

This relationship between class and personal relationships is particularly pronounced in Balzac's fictional world. With deep-rooted hierarchies and social divisions, one's class status determines one's professional or economic position and ability to form meaningful relationships. The era of Balzac has each French citizen sorted into strict categories based on wealth, lineage, and occupation, making the interpersonal relations of that society highly problematic in nature. At the heart of Balzac's study is his depiction of the puzzles and difficulties surrounding romance, family and even friendship between people from different social classes. Social structures and their expectations tend to stand like walls at the core of emotional warmth and proper understanding between people of various backgrounds. These barriers seem to be increased by the chilling presence of the gentry concern, which often leads to disputes and frustration within relationships. Finally, the class relationship does not end with an individual; it is a social phenomenon that affects how characters view and relate to themselves and others in their environment.

The feeling of social class often determines one's self-worth, which in turn affects behaviours and confidence levels. This results in an intricate web in which interpersonal connections transform into metaphors depicting the primary power relations and contests for recognition of the society. Balzac paints a picture of an elephant without glossing over the details of the profoundly complicated power relations embedded within these interactions and captures the strife caused by the collision of social classes. His precise characterisations illustrate the chasm of differences in values, ways of life, and levels of aspirations between people of different social classes and force the audience to question the unquestioned social divides. He then explains how different societal expectations weigh heavily on individuals emotionally, providing a greater understanding of the human condition and how intrinsically we desire to relate and be understood. Ultimately, his writing reveals the psychology of human nature and the need for belonging. Overall, his portrayal remarkably highlights the social structures dictating personal interactions. Balzac has, through fiction, liquidated the boundaries of particularistic social interactions that exist across the lines of social classes.

Aspiration and Mobility: Crossing Boundaries

The idea of aspiration and mobility in Balzac's literary world is deeply embedded in the social structure. People from different strata of society often wish to transcend their limitations and scale the social ladder for reasons such as ambition, love, or the desire to lead a better life. Balzac seems to understand the nuances and difficulties encountered in these pursuits and tries to explain them within the bounds of human nature and the society that enables or limits such actions. Through complex characterisation and elaborate plots, Balzac adeptly portrays the realities of single-minded desperation for social advancement within the confines of class differences that defined his world. Characters often experience the dual suffering of self-aspiration, willfully battling against the restraints imposed on them by society's moral values, which becomes the centre of moral self-examination and ethical self-indulgence. This social exploration is complemented by Balzac's in-depth characterisation, where society's outcasts are examined in the context of their emotions to understand human nature and the drive for self-betterment that defies social convention. In addition, the theme of crossing boundaries involves more than social and class 'mobility.' It integrates borders of geography, culture, and intellect.

Balzac's characters all struggle when entering entirely new layers, whether for economic need, romance, or personal development, seeking the next level. The balance and competition between one's self-driven motives, societal pressures, and the desire to explore new frontiers enable various human aspirations and the desire to go beyond certain limits. Through rich character interactions and complex narratives, Balzac challenges readers to consider the complexities of human ambition in the context of mobility and society. The idea of boundary crossing can be applied to everything Balzac wrote, making his works and statements on human life applicable to any society and type of people, regardless of time and place.

The Human Cost of Social Inequality

Social inequality is a well-known theme in Honoré de Balzac's works due to its relevance to his society and its distinguishing features. By carefully observing the world around him and skillfully narrating it, Balzac explores the effect of inequality in terms of wealth that profoundly impacts people in differing social classes. The struggles between the rich in comfortable positions and the impoverished majority present a platform for discussing human pain and suffering and the will to fight back and overcome trying circumstances.

The impacts of economic inequality are visible throughout Balzac's narratives, and he has carefully crafted the lives of his characters around their aspirations, relationships, and, in essence, how they reflect their fates. At its simplest, economic inequality determines motivation while seeking happiness and self-fulfilment. A key feature of Balzac's work is how different characters struggle with the agony of destitution and are empowered by a ceaseless desire for financial security. A well-defined and constrictive societal framework governs aspiring social climbers' opportunities. It exposes the grim realities of poverty-stricken individuals. Moreover, with great insight, Balzac explains how economic lopsidedness affects human relationships beyond love and family by binding them within the shackles of class and financial need.

Furthermore, the vicious undertones of economic disparity heavily shape the moral ethos of Balzac's world and demonstrate the ethical dilemmas of living in constant poverty. Soliciting wealth through unethical means becomes synonymous with moral degradation, foreshadowing the vices accompanying poverty. On the other hand, the wealthy unshackle themselves from the consequences of compassion and responsibility, yielding to greed and indifference.

Balzac goes beyond the surface to decipher the human heart, describing how economic inequality deprives material and spiritual goods. People's innate dignity and value are often undermined or ignored, resulting in further marginalisation and societal disintegration. Balzac draws readers' attention to the unsettling consequences of economic disharmony, motivating us towards a moral choice and aiding those who suffer from economic injustice while trying to build a more humane society. From all quarters of life that suffer due to economic disparity and its far-reaching repercussions on humanity, he provides us with the dire consequences that stem from it. It is this passionate river view that speaks profoundly in the present age.

His Social Institutions Analysis

While Balzac was a writer, his study of Walpole's life and society should be a reminder that there was not a single facet of social institution that Balzac did not analyse with ruthless precision. Their social institutions were so flawed and hypocritical that the society had given birth to an entire class of people with no intellect. Through actively portraying Sow the People, Balzac repeats the same idea, highlighting the deficiencies of using the syllabic method to learn grammar in primary school.

Whether it is the Northern Boulevards or the Southern districts of Paris, Balzac bravely behaves like a modern-day urban explorer, revealing the underlying moral decline and ethical collapse of commerce and industry. Balzac's piercing critique of the judiciary is one of his most potent. “Lost Illusions” and “Père Goriot” further reveal a world of unscrupulous lawyers and scheming judges who have infested the legal domain with corruption and bribery. His scathing criticism reveals an unjust world where the rich and powerful benefit at the expense of the poor. Balzac does not hesitate to cast the same grim light on a politician as on a judge and banker. With politicians, as with bankers, self-interest and moral decay is the norm. This is achieved through titles such as “A Harlot High and Low” or “The Chouans”.

He exposes a world in which high morals are traded for ruthless assertive politics, hierarchies of power, and self-serving careers. Elaboration suggests that there are constituents of a society whose very existence is suffocated by these egotistical pursuits of dominance and control. Balzac condemns religious institutions and sheds light on the contradictions and failures among the spiritual elite through the complex characters of duplicitous priests and self-serving clergymen in ‘The Country Doctor’ and ‘Eugénie Grandet.’ Balzac paints a picture of a religious authority engrossed in earthly pleasures and sin without regard for the spiritual worthiness they are supposed to practice. Additionally, Balzac does not spare the capitalists and industrialists, revealing the dehumanising consequences of capitalism and industrialisation in his works like 'Eugénie Grandet' and 'The Human Comedy.' The business and trade capitalism world is depicted with cruelty, moral relinquishment, and devastating materialism. The cost of achieving value and status is morally and compassionately inconceivable to them and society. Balzac's work highlights capitalism and success achieved in modern society, as value minus virtue equals negative morality. Balzac's criticism is a powerful reminder of the persistent imperfections and injustices in societies.

Despite our changes, many of his observations remain relevant today. This signifies his importance even in modern-day social structure.

Therefore, Balzac was critical of various precepts and practices adopted by different social institutions. Such phenomena are deeply entrenched within the very fabric of society and often escape the general public's attention. His elaborate characters profoundly showcase the interdependent marvels of social order. With that, Balzac constructs critiques that will resonate with many in the future. Balzac also clarifies that social commentary goes a long way and must be thoroughly examined. He also talks about class strata and how it affects each individual differently. This provides us with an understanding of how social reach can manipulate the fate of an individual. He significantly understood social institutions' immense power on an individual's life, so he remains utterly relevant. Not only does he illustrate class differentiation, but he also provides insightful discourses that aid in understanding the complexities of social settings.

Extracting concepts such as ambition, illusive dreams and moral decay, which is best understood further in detail, allows him to explore the constraining norms these characters have to endure. Through his stories, he highlights the impact of the societal stranglehold and the never-ending struggle to find oneself within the prevailing circumstances. Balzac's work bridges humanity with technology as it not only compels the audience to think deeply but also aids in creating a more profound sense of compassion within them. Readers are urged to ponder the expectations presented within their society since, as his characters do, society rests on a web of features that are pretty intricate. This eliminates the constraint of the season as the discussion is sparked over the repercussions these social structures have on people's expectations, objectives and etiquette. Balzac concludes with an invitation to self-reflect, which dulls the edges of his lasting reflections, allowing them to serve not just as historical perspectives but as a catalyst for actions and further strings of discourse impossible to sever. His narratives, products of a world where individuals exist alongside social structures, serve as mighty recollections, allowing readers to bring forth the deep-rooted truths within the complexities of social commentary.

THE FAILURES AND FORTUNES OF A GENIUS

The Complex Nature of Genius

The intricate nature of genius is like a puzzle with missing pieces. Honoré de Balzac brilliantly articulates this. Balzac struggled with several personal setbacks and societal feuds, which starkly contrasted with his unparalleled genius. Balzac's mastery of weaving elaborate tales and dynamic character construction was nothing short of remarkable. Balzac was a true literary genius; however, his tumultuous personal life deeply affected him and left a mark on his psyche. The harrowing situations he faced during his formative years moulded Balzac's worldview and drove him to pursue literary excellence. The juxtaposition of adversity and unparalleled genius in Balzac's life elucidates the delicate relationship between chaos and creativity. As we analyse his personal struggles and creative process deeper, it becomes clear that the intricacies of Balzac's genius go beyond mere literary acuity.

The fragility and flaws in his psyche shaped a profound background on which Balzac's masterpieces were created. The complexities surrounding genius are beautifully articulated in Balzac's life.

In Honoré de Balzac's life, as in many great authors, a decisive moment led to many struggles and hardships for him. This moment occurs in his adolescence, and for one to understand this aspect of Balzac's life, one must look at the years that shaped him before he became a published author. To say that Balzac had a difficult life is an understatement; for an artist of his calibre, he faced many struggles. On May 20, 1799, Balzac was born in Tours, France, where, as a child, he had to endure a lot of pain. His father passed away untimely when he was just eight, throwing the family into chaos. Instability and plunging debts were the family norm, setting the author up for chronic economic hardship. With the death of his father, his mother tried to educate him the best she could, which further developed his intelligence while also nurturing his love for literature.

Even today, Balzac has little formal educational training, and he had many academic challenges as a youth. The determination to overcome these challenges drove him to immerse himself in a turbulent path that ultimately turned him into a well-known novelist. Balzac faced similar obstacles during his business ventures. His investments in publishing and trade often ended in financial loss, further intensifying the connection between his difficulties and the myriad of characters struggling with similar predicaments in his novels. Undoubtedly, these encounters developed his understanding of socioeconomic relations, and they motivated him to write from a first-person perspective. Such relentless struggles created a feeling of authenticity that was magnified through personal suffering. Balzac faced further challenges when trying to break through as a playwright, as his plays received little public interest. Though he was depressed by this stage of unfulfilled expectations, it did force Balzac to come to terms with many stringent realities in the field of creativity and, subsequently, mainstream fiction. This shift allowed him to begin writing his most significant publication, La Comédie Humaine.

The trials and tribulations that Balzac encountered will undoubtedly help the reader gain a deeper understanding of his unwavering dedication towards his work. Balzac's early years were filled with struggle that heavily impacted him; his performance in the attempt to understand human suffering was deeply affected, and contextually, his style was raw and unrefined. All of this paints a deeper picture of why his creativity continued blooming. Over the years, Balzac developed an eagle-like focus towards literature, building and sustaining a comprehensive understanding of the world, which was the catalyst that allowed him to drive his struggles into a fountain of inspiration.

Balzac's financial stresses throughout his life were something of an ever-present shadow. Balzac's debt was on the verge of overwhelming and constantly threatened his stability as a writer. Balzac's life was filled with successes, but time and time again, he fell deeper into a pit of financial turmoil. The debt he was burdened under was endless, alongside the pressure of commercial success and paying off creditors while maintaining a semblance in society. Balzac's life paints a tragic tale of struggle and strife, the era of literature where he truly shone.

Not only did this struggle take a great amount of his time and energy, but it also affected the themes and plots of his writing. Balzac's financial situation, which was very delicate, also had noteworthy repercussions on his life. It caused strains in his relationships, intense anxiety and stress, as well as severe isolation to escape the possibilities of financial distress. This environment must have had a profound and lasting impact on Balzac's mind, which, in return, affected the characters and nature he created in his novels and stories. Moreover, Balzac's creative work was also greatly influenced, directly and indirectly, by economic burdens. Being perpetually in debt meant he had to work at an unprecedented level to escape these relentless demands, which ultimately enlarged his body of work. While such ideas and themes indulged Balzac, they also raised questions regarding how much his artistic vision was compromised due to such intense financial demands. This strain left his vision warped and made him relentlessly remove parts of his work, which profoundly altered his insight into the human condition.

Exploring the world of financial devastation and its widespread repercussions allows us to untangle the web comprised of different elements of Balzac's life and art. Balzac's life reveals his understanding of these obstacles and his determination to rise above the challenges, and his dedication serves as a motivating force. While he was grappling with financial difficulties, he accomplished remarkable literary ballets that captured the hearts of readers and cemented his standing as one of the literary sphere's geniuses.

Achievements

Honoré de Balzac is known for several notable achievements in the realm of fiction, positioning him as one of the leading figures in realistic fiction. In addition, the ability to dissect human behaviour and intricately weave them into engaging tales places him as one of the practitioners of fiction in his era. Balzac painted an intriguing picture of imagination mixed with realism, depicting various aspects of life, which appealed to readers and earned him fame. He is revered in modern society because of the significant impact that his fascinating storytelling has had on the world. Balzac's enduring work, 'La Comédie Humaine,' is a hallmark of his legacy.

This sprawling project was a set of interrelated novels and short stories that provided an all-encompassing view of French society in the 1800s. Every piece woven into this complex work encapsulates the greatest aspects of human life through its characters, themes, and locations. The scope and detail within 'La Comédie Humaine' show Balzac's unwavering dedication to capturing the many sides of life with absolute honesty, unrelenting. Balzac paid careful attention to even the most minor details of the work's setting, characters, and emotions. Thus, his vivid prose style significantly changed how novels came to be treated as an art form. By abandoning preconceived notions of characters and adopting true realism, Balzac showcased that literature could serve as a lens to society, showcasing its good and bad equally without bias. To those hoping to transform the craft of fiction, his novel approach to storytelling proves to be motivational. It serves as an inspiration to this day. Balzac's ability to craft compelling and realistic multi-dimensional characters has, time and time again, revolutionised how literature is written.

Starting with the enchanting Rastignac from 'Le Père Goriot' to the moving titular figures in 'Eugénie Grandet' and 'Père Goriot,' Balzac brought to life an impressive range of characters, all of whom possessed the unmistakable traits of a real person. His meticulous studies of human nature, along with their plans, wish, and eventual disillusionment, brought unheard-of richness to his characters, making them believable for readers of every age. Through his literary success, Balzac managed to go above the limitations of time and place, sculpting his characters in the soul of every person.

In one sentence, Balzac's victories in literature prove his unrivalled creativity and unparalleled influence on the world. It's profoundly reasoned and understood that helps him gain that reputation from other writers because he expresses the complex nature of a human, making him one of the greatest writers of all time.

The Conflict Between Balzac's Personal Goals and His Reality

As we know, Balzac, a writer of his time, was renowned for his writing skills, and, as most would know, he had marvellous personal goals. He yet struggled with the chaos of everyday life. The strong wish to achieve notoriety sought after in literature was intense and often fuelled his life with a cranky, stubborn attitude that did not help him when trying to make a name for himself in the writing world.

The idea he had in his mind vastly differed from the idealised image he held and the realities he was forced to confront. While sailing through the rough waters of the publishing business and societal expectations, he faced challenges unaligned with his aspirations. Even if he was sure of his talent and vision, Balzac constantly battled financial issues, social contempt, and the constant fear of irrelevance. Through his life and work, the harsh restraints on him culminated in the never-ending friction he experienced between his self-esteem and perception. In addition, the boundaries he faced to make money and achieve fame often battled with his desire to create art and express himself. Compounding this reality was the effect of Balzac's love life and the emotional bonds he forged, which complicated the relationship between his goal and the unyielding realities of life he faced. He had to constantly fight between professional obligations to create literary works of the highest calibre and his desire to feel companionship. This tussle resulted in him experiencing immense internal conflict—one that placed his passions against responsibility, which altered the way he wrote and made their impact agitating and passionate, something readers still cherish today. Balzac indeed displayed resilience and adaptability, but only to get through the tight space between his hopes and the circumstances that limited him.

Every writer embodies the spirit of progress not through their pen alone but through the mental anguish of grappling with failures at every step. Indeed, Balzac's life proves that when someone is determined to achieve something, they will push through all obstacles and, time and again, break the barrier of failures, rejections, and, dare I say, mental breakdowns. What is striking is how polished the prose is – refreshing even! Each chapter stirred up some emotion, some a baffling anger, rage, and sadness. In contrast, others touched me delicately like a feather. What followed was so positive and inspiring that it compelled me to think about blending passion and ambition with life, serving as a canvas on which art is painted. Balzac always held onto an idealistic vision of life through a naive lens that shattered to pieces when met with reality. This dance between his inner thoughts, profound ideas, and the world around him gave life a whole new essence. These masterpieces argue why art and reality went hand in hand, and this is why Balzac is unforgettable in the world of literature, where he helped redefine the nature of words and prose. Balzac provides a breathtaking masterpiece full of lessons spruced with emotions, offering everyone an insight into the wonders of the interplay between humanity and life.

The Effect of Failure on Growth in Artistry Balzac's life provides a clear example of how failure can impact one's goals in a significant manner. Deconstructing each hurdle becomes an intricate design of effort and investment, leading to disappointment and struggle. This complex matrix has different outcomes, resulting in the repetition of disheartening experiences with many negative consequences. Accomplishments, on the other hand, distil motivation, acting as a catalyst for transformation and positive progression. Balzac's failures provided hostility that compelled him to nurture new forms of creativity. A surge of motivation and intrinsic discontent allowed great artists like Balzac to harness inspiration encapsulated through defeat, which was a building block to novel creation. Berated by society's expectations, Balzac's literary works created a new frontier showcasing raw portrayal of society's most profound failures juxtaposed with high aspirations. Great art certainly draws in myriad emotions and feelings, all directed at providing catharsis for an artist's struggles and pain. In turn, transcending defeat into art serves to deepen and enrich Balzac's literary collection viscerally. This loss extraction allows fresh realism without distorting the core of art. Alongside realism, it affords freedom to the bolstering emotions encompassing the work. Lastly, Balzac was immensely aided by failure, which was directed towards resolving his ideologies and perception of social culture. Balzac's comprehensive diction allowed him to build empathy in the eyes of readers, pulling them towards his pieces. All while enabling them to realise their stark reality.

He explored the intricacies of human development and motivation when confronted with challenges. He created characters that captured the paradoxical and delicate nature of people. Balzac weaved the lessons learned from failure into the narrative loom of his works, which ultimately transformed his literary skill and the profound depths of his work. Balzac can also be understood as a man who had a thirst to attend to and sculpt the disconnected pieces of his works. This disconnection stems from the early pieces of literature that received dismissive and even violent critiques. Balzac never regarded criticism as a setback; he welcomed it with open arms, and by doing so, he could unlock newer realms of creativity. This newfound approach allowed Balzac to tame this newfound barrage of hatred and transform it into admiring work that most readers still cherish today. In conclusion, the incorporation of pieces of brilliance in his entire body of work and the approach towards and the aftermath of failure were essential to Balzac. An onslaught from all directions leading towards him resulted in unshackling the limitless depths of his imagination.

Balzac's ability to turn failures into literary gold speaks volumes about failure's drastic effect on creativity. His life resonates with and inspires many upcoming and established authors.

Balzac's Relationship with Critics and Peers

As a highly regarded and influential writer of his time, Honoré De Balzac's pieces of literature were always open to scrutiny by contemporaries, critics, and fellow writers. His writings were met with mixed feelings and responses that ranged from praise to intense revolt, which depicts how controversial Balzac was in the literary domain. In his social life, Balzac's interactions with critics and peers, like many authors of his time, had other sides, such as fascination, hostility and even envy. Encountering many views and opinions, Balzac walked the thin line of scepticism towards his challengers and respect for supporters, balancing his stance and showing vulnerability while remaining strong. A significant reason for Balzac's defences towards critical evaluations was his prior experience of foment descriptors associated with doubt alongside one of gaining fans. Balzac refrained from taking such assessment at face value, and such an approach helped him avoid being simple-minded.

Moreover, Balzac's peers and their relationships showcase the nuances of artistic collaboration and rivalry in the 19th century. The French author Balzac had many friendships and rivalries with several essential writers of the time, like George Sand, Victor Hugo, and Alexandre Dumas, who were all, in some ways, peers, friends, and rivals simultaneously. Their letters and recorded meetings are evidence of the rich interplay of ideas, arguments, and well-mannered confrontations that were a feature of Paris's literary salons and circles at that time. Despite the unavoidable clashes that stemmed from wanting to achieve different visionary goals and having personal objectives, literature remained the centre of balance for Balzac. Such interactions benefited Balzac greatly throughout his career, and simultaneously, Balzac shaped the literary culture of the period through these relationships. Balzac had different relationships with critics and peers, and these differing relationships shed light on the conflicting aspects of his literary voice. It demonstrates the depth of his works on the intellectual life of his times and the strife of some acclaim and some condemnation of his art. Further, it serves as a powerful snapshot of the world behind the text, stressing the relativity of all literature to human relationships and, in turn, the human impact on the literary world.

Understanding Public Perception

Public perception is an important feature of any art practitioner's career, and this remains equally true for Honoré de Balzac.

From the start of his career, Balzac showed an astute understanding of governance and politics, crucial for his success and fame. Balzac had an unyielding dedication to portraying the coexistence and relationships in life. At the onset of his career, the reactions to his work were relatively divided. While some praised his remarkable depiction of reality and unique style, others criticised his controversial narratives as needlessly provocative. Balzac's writing enabled him to embrace the incredibly intricate nature of humanity, meaning that Balzac's relationship with public perception was complex. Balzac's early encounters with public perception shaped his understanding of varying audiences. Subsequently, they changed how he wrote in the future. These changes enabled Balzac to understand the ever-changing society he was a part of and mould his writing to best fit the atmosphere. André Gide more concisely stated, "To my contemporaries, I chose to make myself inert." His enigmatic persona, characterised by a blend of ambition, introspection, and occasional reclusiveness, allowed Balzac to encapsulate audiences while creating mystery, inviting brushes.

Balzac's public image was shaped by the scope of his self-representation and the public expectations attached to it—this, in turn, moulded the relationship he maintained with his readers and critics. He slowly began to pay attention to the social implications of his words. Balzac's La Comédie Humaine, arguably his masterpiece, put him under much public scrutiny and changed how he perceived the creative process. Because he aimed to capture the essence of human reality, he integrated himself and his work into the ever-changing public sentiment. He was able to walk the fine line that existed between public admiration and scorn, and in doing so, was able to develop his public persona and artistic vision further. To wrap up, Balzac's dealings with his public simplify the nature of the relationship between Balzac as an artist and the people who consumed his art. His reputation undoubtedly started changing with time, and this concept captures the essence of Balzac's head-spinning life. His ability to stay true to his art during the harshest criticism while shifting public opinion shows why his influence will never fade and why his meditation will always remain relevant.

Coping Mechanisms and Resilience

Honoré de Balzac's story illustrates how overarching suffering between Babylonian myths and realities allowed him to articulate the struggles his sophisticated characters faced. The need for a creative reprieve was often felt as a forced release through his written narratives. Despite confining pressures, his ability to ground his work in the rawness of human experience gave rise to poignant tales that resonated with readers. He was noted for his remarkable ability to write complex characters steeped in life's intricacies as they navigated numerous societal challenges. An influential figure offered varied viewpoints on creating engaging plots that could lead readers through a maze of artistic exploration, portraying themes of hardship, emotional strife, and ultimate triumph.

While in despair, Balzac relied on storytelling as his love for it acted as a therapeutic outlet in channelling his emotional pain into vivid narratives that resonate with countless people worldwide, absolutely testifying to the healing power of literature. Furthermore, Balzac showed great personal strength by persisting through challenges without allowing them to sidetrack his creativity. His unfaltering grit enabled him to endure the turbulence caused by extreme criticism and rejection and offer his body and soul to further enthusiasm for his craft. Moreover, his ability to draw from the suffering of a personal nature and mould that into incredible works of literature tells of the indefatigable spirit underpinning all of his work. In addition, Balzac's resilience is exemplified by his ability to seek comfort from social interactions through a supportive network to bolster his confidence during tough times. His fictional characters served as sources of inspiration, teaching him invaluable lessons that strengthened his determination and helped him survive in harsh environments. Most importantly, Balzac's power to his characters showcases literary resilience's profound impact on an individual's spirit during hardship.

Success Evaluation: Retrospective Analysis Examination

During our examination of Balzac's accomplishments, it is clear that his life and literary career were both highly successful and burdened with great suffering.

To grasp his success in sheer metrics, one must remember the impact of his work on the world of literature, the adversity he faced, and the relevance of his themes. Balzac's success was measured in literary pieces, as well as the complexity and amount of societal issues prevalent at that time. His legacy is rooted in his ability to portray French society and the multifaceted aspects of human nature. Even though he is remembered for his humanitarian struggles, coming out and succeeding in a highly adversarial environment depicts remarkable willpower. In addition, because his legacy is arguably one of the most controversial emerging writers of French literature, there is an evident need for it to be evaluated and contextualised compared to his contemporaries. A divided reception of conflicts and controversies as a backdrop during his life provides insight into his character. However, over time, his genius appeals to people and readers across the globe, and his position strengthens as a dominant figure in literature. These traits are passed along with his insights on societal structures, aiding modern-day critiques and scholars in understanding his literature. Furthermore, along with the other angles, consideration should be given to the importance of the literary heritage left by Balzac in juxtaposition with other writers, critics, and thinkers who came after him.

The impact of his innovative approaches to stories told, his harsh realistic portrayal of extreme human desires, and his brutal social criticism is profoundly felt to this day. These novelists, Emile Zola, Charles Dickens, and Marcel Proust, were further magnified by Balzac's success in setting the standards of story writing. Lastly, no general survey of Balzac's success could be truly understood without outlining the physical and mental exhaustion his pursuit of incomparable artistic standards brought on. The sacrifices he made to achieve such success, the personal and professional obstacles he faced, and the unending battle with obscurity all vastly aid in portraying a more complete picture of him. Balzac is a master in understanding and creating works of literature that reflect the life of his time, and this vividly explains the complexity of his achievements. In conclusion, the analyses conducted on Balzac's success show not only the strong effect his works had on readers throughout the ages but also that the man himself and the reasons behind his mastery are far more complex and eloquent than he set out to be. The combination of where he started, how he is viewed now, and everything in between paints an alluring illustrative picture and justifies him as a literary great whose works surpassed the limits of time and continue to be treasured by readers and writers alike.

THE FEMALE QUESTION: HEROINES AND HUMAN DEPTH

Women's Contribution in Balzac's Narrative Universe

With unparalleled human insight, Balzac masterfully chronicles the intricate identity matrix of women in society. The conflict between social norms and the stereotypical behavioural spectrum of women serves as the crux of the complexity in which he depicts his female characters. Through his tactic of literary analysis, Balzac adeptly shies away from referring to social culture as a restriction and instead shifts his focus towards the stronger desires, virtues, and vices of the idolised women in his novels. He vividly narrates the social, emotional, and psychological complexity of womanhood, which is incorporated into his female characters. In pursuing such motifs, Balzac destroys the dominant conceptualisation of the phenomenon of womanhood. Balzac's heroines articulate some of the many successes and challenges that stem from the selfless and ambitious to the devoutly moral and ruthlessly cynical. Theodora, Claire, and Petronilla are doers, and their actions stem from external expectations and internal desires, making them multi-dimensional and timeless.

Balzac illustrates the continuous struggle and tenacity of those attempting to achieve independence, love, and self-actualisation by focusing on the shifting statuses of women in 19th-century France. His profound knowledge of psychology and sociology enables Balzac to delve deeper into the narrative possibilities and fundamental intricacies of female characters that profoundly affect the themes within his literature.

Balzac's Approaches to Feminine Ethos

Diverse in the classification of heroine types, the literary works of Honoré de Balzac reflect the social life and different aspects of humanity that he so intensely focused on. From the deep analysis of Balzac's works, it is easy to note that these women function as the primary instruments or characters that show the nature and behaviour of people and the changes in women's status in France during the 19th century. Focusing his analysis on Balzac's writings helps us understand the different facets of femininity and how these females influenced Balzac's thematic concerns prominently. In his examined works, Balzac's heroines defy labels as they present a new, albeit sensational, combination of good and bad character traits, desires, and weaknesses. Each represents their corresponding archetype based on Balzac's semiotic theorised society in which personal freedom is married with external subjugation, analysing the existential dilemma of women during his time.

Ranging from the striking Eugénie Grandet to the elusive Madame de Mortsauf, Balzac's protagonists are remarkable for the variety of their apparent motives and the moral conflicts they engage in. Beyond the archetypes themselves, there are layers of incredible depth that reflect the author's deep empathy for the intricacies of the female condition. Balzac's female characters were never merely props that served a plot; they were fully fleshed individuals with emotional, psychological, and mental complexity who stepped outside the boundaries of literature. These women with internal struggles, aspirations, and successes illustrate the remarkable depth of femininity against the backdrop of post-revolutionary France. From this perspective, it becomes clear why Balzac's work remains responsive to contemporary readers. His works embody the struggles of gender identity, societal expectations, and changes that every modernised nation experiences, making his heroines relatable and timeless icons.

Feminine Virtue and Vice: A Complex Dichotomy

In the complex folds of Balzac's fiction, the idea of a double standard of feminine virtue and vice combines to form a striking Balzacian Paradox that exposes the intricacies of vice. Through these characters, Balzac constructed stereotypes that combine virtue and vice with incredible nuance, profoundly challenging the tussle between morality and immorality.

The depiction of femininity in Balzac's works critiques traditional societal standards and ventures into human psychology. In Balzac's tales, a woman's virtue is a blend of loyalty, kindness, and bravery, as shown by the characters Eugénie Grandet and Madame de Mortsauf, who triumphed over their life's challenges. Grandet and Mortsauf's endurance against adversities redefines femininity beyond its shallow constructs, making them moral paragons. On the other hand, Balzac uses femme fatales like Delphine de Nucingen and Valerie Marneffe to explain womanly vice. By replacing stereotypical villains with deeply flawed humans, Balzac showcases complex characters who abandon morality to pursue desires and ambitions. Balzac captures the struggles of the human mind with a deft touch that unveils the frailties and contradictions that all of us battle with. This duality of feminine virtue and vice reveals a critical commentary on the human experience that transcends gender.

The best of Balzac's novels reveal his characteristic realism and emotional intensity through the heroes and heroines of his stories. His fully fleshed characters are rounded in every way. They all possess inner conflicts, uncertainty, intense feelings, and promising ambitions. Feeling love, intense passion, overwhelming jealousy, and excruciating despair are the emotions that drive Balzac's characters towards reaching the depths and pinnacles of what humanity encapsulates. As readers, we are empowered with intimate insights into his characters' turmoil, inner desires, and motivations. His words do not merely venture far and wide in search of humans; instead, they extend deeply and profoundly into their emotions, teaching us that home doesn't always have to mean a tangible structure filled with things but rather a self-defined conceptual space that invites, rests, and provides comfort.

Balzac's Psychological Realism was evident through his characters and plot diagrams. By imbuing richly multifaceted characters, he ensured that he did not simply craft plot puppets but built fleshed-out characters with phenomenal emotional depth. Such complexity enables the audience to empathise with the characters' experiences and struggles, creating a deep connection with the narrative. In addition, Balzac's emotional depth goes beyond individual character portrayal towards the general theme of humanity's nature and society. Balzac's strongly constructed insight into human psychology allows him to break down society's constructs and norms to reveal the emotion that motivates human behaviour in a particular social setting. Through psychological realism, Balzac does not merely construct a story but instead creates a window for readers to contemplate their emotional experiences and interpersonal relationships. Lastly, the emotional depth fictionalised in Balzac's work serves as a reminder of the universality of human emotion. Balzac's ability to capture complexity with a timeless essence enables readers from all generations and societies to appreciate his work.

Balzac is perpetually identified as one of the greatest complexities of humanity and literature because of his masterful expressiveness and psychological intricacy.

Balzac's Influences – Contextual History and the Subjective Lens

Honoré de Balzac was a celebrated author of the nineteenth century and was heavily shaped by the context of history and his subjective lenses. He was born in an era of significant change across France, surging during the impact of the French Revolution and the reign of Napoleon Bonaparte. The consequences of such impactful events would guide his perception of the world and influence his writings. Further, Balzac's subjective life experience shaped how he integrated various themes into his writing. His life of chasing a certain social status while contending with debt appears through several of his characters' struggles. These characters in his books reflect the intricate way he tackles relationships, social power struggles, and the societal framework of France. All these assumptions manifest in his perception and experience of French society. Not to forget, his attention towards history, especially when Napoleon was in power, shaped his writings and allowed him to accurately depict the characters and the settings in his vivid portrayals.

His accounts illustrate his unfiltered art as they encompass everything, from the debaucheries of the opulent elites to the abject poverty of the lower classes. Balzac's gender and class biases are also evident in his writings. His central characters focus on the harsh boundaries and expectations set up by society, which reveals not only societal attitudes but also the realities of it. The gender discrimination, the class gap, and the unforgiving rat race of social stratification serve as the haunting melody of most of his works. Balzac's ability to intertwine fact with fiction defines his work; his stories touch on elements of untimely human struggles, such as societal context and personal bias. With the sharpness of his observations and the depth of his analysis of the human psyche, Balzac captures readers' hearts every day and in every era.

Societal Expectations v. Reality vs Personal Aspirations

It is clear from the reading of Honoré de Balzac that social obligations significantly interfere with the passions and endeavours of his female characters. As a careful observer of social behaviours, Balzac deals profoundly with the social fabric and its effects on individual aspirations, especially about women in 19th-century France. Balzac's heroines face a great irony of society's expectations against their personal needs and consequences. Further, Foucauldian analysis of the heritage of Balzac brings to light the conflicts that stem from the heady mix of family expectation, social responsibility and personal ambition. He shows how these oppositions contour and define the experiences of his female characters and why the experiences are so richly textured and variegated. Amid the dictatorship of social aspirations, Balzac's heroines struggle with personal goals that are socially and gender-wise confined. These opposing conditions create the most interesting and complex images that explain the phenomena of the fulfilment or unfulfillment of goals on the personal and social levels.

By setting the social boundaries against the passions and aspirations of his female characters, Balzac highlights the challenges they undergo while simultaneously providing essential insights regarding the socio-cultural structure of his era. Therefore, Balzac's social and self-imposed challenges are depicted as an arduous fight for freedom, self-fulfilment, and self-empowerment within the deep-seated folds of society. This aspect of Balzac's work is one of the reasons why many consider him to be a champion of the human experience, who, unlike many artists, appeals to various audiences, both now and in the future.

Vautrin, Eugénie Grandet, and Madame de Mortsauf

In a profound analysis of femininity and the feminist perspective of Honoré de Balzac's literature and works, there stand out a few characters that serve as perfect case studies for a woman's role in the French society of the early 19th century. Vautrin is a cunning and brilliant character who adopts several different roles and dresses as a man to challenge society's acceptance of women. Balzac uses Vautrin to interrogate gender identity and the social limitations placed upon people. In contrast, there is also Eugénie Grandet, a woman who carries Balzac's name as the title of her novel and whose character defines the fight for freedom and individuality against the oppressive systems of the family and patriarchy. Her life story poignantly recounts the strife between personal goals and societal expectations, depicting the grief too many women endure while seeking autonomy in a suffocating society.

When examining female agency and economic independence, Honoré de Balzac approaches the discussion by scrutinising women's lives in a society with harsh gendered norms and an economy that limits them. Balzac's heroines are often bound to patriarchal structures, but the most astonishing part is their ability to overcome such obstacles. Through his craft, Balzac grapples with the contradictions of self-sustainable women and the realities of changing times. This tension for autonomy is perhaps most pronounced in the characters of Eugénie Grandet and Madame de Restaud, who try to manage the privileges of their family's societal wealth combined with the constraints that come with it. These women face undue societal pressures and, as a result, reflect profoundly on the multitude of constraints cast upon them on account of being women. Balzac captures their struggles as they seek to attain self-identity in a society where economic self-reliance is considered a luxury meant for men and illustrates how determined women become in pursuit of such goals.

This balance is vital in dissecting the thematic tapestry done by Balzac's work since it highlights reasonable commentary on women's economic power relations. Moreover, the character of Vautrin provides an interesting challenge to the balance of gender relations as presented in Balzac's works. Vautrin's economically motivated cross-dressing and subversion of the existing gender relations norm suggests a more complex understanding of agency and autonomy, making one ponder the social order. In addition, Vautrin's cross-dressing and pursuit of economic affluence suggest a bold challenge to the stereotyped subordinate status of women and provide a new outlook towards freedom. Even so, the changing heroines of Balzac mark a brilliant attempt to illustrate the interaction between the socio-economic position of a person and their freedom. These women, with a focus on marriage, inheritance and other business dealings, represent the constant struggle for independence from economic dictatorship. In the setting of economic oppression and the traditional values of mid-19th century France, Balzac tells a story relevant to current debates around gender and financial independence. In studying the comprehensive facets of women's economic power relations, Balzac asks readers to think about what is clear and relevant in today's world.

Analysing the Negative Side From a Contemporary Standpoint

While criticising Balzac's depiction of women, contemporary critics have raised some intriguing points that demand careful examination.

A common criticism is the depiction of female characters as primarily determined by their relations with men or as mere objects to be acted upon. This view shows the underlying power relations and gendered inequalities embedded in Balzac's stories, revealing how women are placed about male actions as though they do not matter. Another critical point of contention is the lack of agency that characterises many of Balzac's female characters, especially in his later work, whose fate seems to be inescapably linked to the prevailing social and patriarchal order. While some of them are shown to exhibit some degree of spirit and defiance, as most critics agree, their destinies are ineluctably bound to the actions of the males around them or other greater forces. Furthermore, modern studies evaluate the moral issues of Balzac's portrayal of women consigned to subservient positions about their husband's affection for them and their capacity for self-advancement. These discourses raise the question of how his female characters respond to sociocultural demands or whether their actions—if any—are free or excessively regulated by the mandate of the prevailing patriarchal society. In addition, writers and scholars still have more interest in the relationship between class, gender, and power in Balzac's works concerning women.

Critics delve into the differences in agency, access, and social roles of the characters based on their class, demonstrating the intersection of gender violence and social class in Balzac's world. Modern analyses, however, question whether the multitude of roles and layers within Balzac's heroines go beyond typical literary tropes and if his works adequately reflect the range of realities and complexities different women experience. This set of questions illustrates the transformations in understanding feminist literary criticism and, more importantly, the shifts that broadened the scope of women's literature beyond heretofore existing paradigms. As a diverse set of voices emerge, these critical discussions reveal that contemporary scholarship no longer solely focuses on revisiting Balzac's representation of women but recognises his work as significant in understanding scholarship on gender, identity, and agency as well.

Conclusion: Balzac's Heroines and Their Enduring Impact

Balzac's heroines' impact remains a fundamental aspect of contemporary culture, and we understand this through the author's deep grasp of human nature. Examining today's complex world, one can appreciate Balzac's female characters and their struggles even more deeply. These unforgettable heroines serve as the embodiment of humanity and the multi-dimensional oppressions society casts.

This persistent impact does not depart from literature but encompasses the more excellent conversation about gender, agency, and sociology. The development of feminist thought and the study of gender relations have upheld the place of Balzac's heroines as pivotal elements in the history of women's literature. Their indomitable spirit, strength, and ability to struggle within a patriarchal society make them harrowing prototypes of what is still the striving for gender justice. In addition, the subtleties of Balzac's heroines illuminate the depths of human nature, which is vital for discussions about identity, representation, and empowerment. Balzac's women also reflect the literary vision, which endows these characters with a value that does not diminish with age. Unsurprisingly, Balzac's characters continue to inspire novels, plays, and even films, suggesting that they serve as a central text for cultural discourse. These variations, like Balzac's heroines, are broader than the book. The adaptation of dramas and even films retells Balzac's literature further, extending the impact Balzac's work has had on the public today. In short, the modern effect of Balzac's heroines is the primary didactic example that serves every period, country, and its citizens best. Literature can make anything a reality, and thus, it prompts self-contemplation and reflection.

While trying to understand the intricacies of gender, identity, and social structures, Balzac's heroines deepen our understanding of human strength and complexity. This further enhances the literary world and sustains the dialogue on gender, power, and the unending quest for balance on all fronts.

DEBT, DESIRE, AND THE DRIVE FOR CREATION

Struggles With Personal and Financial Matters of Balzac

Balzac suffers as a significant debt stakeholder, constantly struggling to pay his debts since he can never gain authentic commercial value from his work. Balzac, sometimes perceived as one of the world's foremost novelists of the 19th century, was perpetually in financial trouble, owing his financial troubles to his debts, which stemmed from his spending habits and his lifestyle. Balzac paid towards servicing his debts through the earnings from the body of work that he produced. Much of his debt always raised the burden over his day-to-day activities, constraining his existence into perpetual hopelessness. These struggles affected not only his commercial endeavours but also his personal life and ability to write. The perpetual search for a balance that would allow him to teach himself as an author of noble standing during his time forced him into an elaborate set of systems where he used debt to generate creative outputs in search of solvency. The continuous want and fulfilment created an artificial market as his reputation single-handedly pushed the balance to its peak. As a result of these strains, Balzac wrote extensively, as writing in varying conditions enabled him to unleash new metaphors and simultaneously secure his position in the market.

Furthermore, Balzac's financial troubles had an impact on his relationships, as well as his emotional and psychological state. The worrying demand for the money owed to him flowed back into his relationships with colleagues and associates, poisoning the experience even in the optimistic moments of happiness and success. The blend of financial struggles and personal pain gave the thematic core of his literary works a more profound and richer meaning, providing a rough and unrefined representation of the human condition and the struggle to survive. In a single stroke, the connections between creativity, struggle and an artist's undying need to express themselves become clearer and provide insight into Balzac's life – a facet that begs to be explored. Considering the drastic consequences of financial doom on Balzac's mental state and career, there is more to be understood about such powerful forces that drove his narrative skills and marvel at the wondrous mix of deeply personal pain and unexplored territories of surpassing boundaries in literature.

In Debt's Context – The Motivation for Creation

Debt, which is usually regarded as restrictive, can shape the creative drive, especially for artists. Honoré de Balzac's case is clear: throughout his life, he faced financial concerns; however, debt seemed to encourage him to produce more written work over time.

The burden of financial obligations and creditors' threats might seem like an impediment to creative expression. Nonetheless, for Balzac, this was a source of motivation that drove him towards accomplishing success, so the pursuit never ceased. This oscillation and interplay between financial indebtedness and motivation for art is curious and certainly deserves inquiry. Indeed, stress from economic liabilities can serve as a motivation for creators to work towards something meaningful. For instance, Balzac's pile of debt made it necessary to write so extensively that it even masked the limits of his imagination. Every word written served as a stepping stone towards putting the mountain of obligations to rest. The pen, for Balzac, transformed into a liberating instrument. The quest for self-creative satisfaction came into a duel with tremendous financial responsibilities that led to an internal conflict, which shifted the entire balance of his work. In addition, financial obligations can also enable innovation and risk-taking. With the instability of finance lingering over his head, Balzac stepped into the unknown and pushed boundaries concerning narrative style and themes. Financial risk deficit was a guiding and convincing incentive to take contrarian positions in literature and explore raw emotions that were traditionally never touched. This complex relationship between debt and creativity is a key aspect of Balzac's life and work that warrants further exploration.

By doing this, he transformed the challenges of innovation into the unlimited potential of creativity-rich opportunities, which, in turn, expanded the borders of literature, and telling stories became more intricate. In particular, Balzac's debts affected not only his writing style but also the content of his writings. These authors are battling financial turmoil, which is further complicated by societal pressure and a sense of ethics, and they end up being brutally realistic in their storytelling. Through his skilful desecration of the human psyche bound in the shackles of limited finances, Balzac escalated the level of discussion on social injustices and human weakness and went on to do more than tell stories in response to the ever-changing shifts of humanity. In short, creative motivation stemming from debt effectively examines the relationship between struggle and imagination. Balzac demonstrated how burdens of finances can uncontrollably transform motives into means, and from the fire of relentless debt, echoing literature was born. So his name shall be remembered by future readers.

A Want as a Means to Attain Literature Deed

A want that has led to changes and rewrites of such complexity that no one ever fathomed would, sits planted as the reason behind literary delicacies as a want led to some of the greatest achievements of mankind.

For example, consider Honoré de Balzac, who I believe possessed an inner core of ambition that significantly shaped his workplace endeavours. The single purpose of preserving his name within the cluster of renowned writers motivated Balzac to work continuously in crafting his desired masterpiece titled La Comédie Humaine. This faint desire, whose foundation stems from a never-ending desire to live forever, manifested through artistic work, motivated Balzac time and time again. This strong motivational force was deeply engrained within him. Yet, it was intertwined with human feelings, cultural interactions and a deeper questioning of one's own existence, which explains the underlying beauty within his work. Composed of Balzac's dreams and ideas, his perfected characters encapsulate the blend of human emotion, revealing their deeper complexities and how unobtrusive they allow to be uncovered. Balzac portrayed this moral struggle between aspirations, needs, and ethical boundaries in Eugène de Rastignac, Goriot, and other characters he featured, graphically displaying nature's delicate crown jewels. Beyond his fictional world, Balzac's imagination opened the door to the world of his personal life and professional ambitions, where the most profound desire rested.

His relentless search for success and prominence showed how penetrative passion could be in his creative exploits. Desiring wealth, Balzac focused on material possessions while neglecting essential aspects of his life and dealing with severe financial troubles. Additionally, the desire was blatant in his entrepreneurial activity. Balzac's rather alarming literary output was greatly informed by the economic needs he sought to fulfil, which furthers the discussion on why aspiration played a key role in the invention of the work. Therefore, for Balzac, desire, when shown in its most extreme form, acted as the treasure box he unlocked using the key with which he carved his name into eternity.

Art and Economic Challenges

The inescapable economic challenges of his time drastically altered and shaped Balzac's life and his work, both as an artist and a writer. Even within these hardships of life, writing was an avenue for Balzac to express himself, and due to his financial problems, he found creativity easy. With a desperate need for money and the weight of debt on his shoulders, the artist combined his economic needs with his creativity.

With Balzac's astute analysis, the effects brought forth by the economy were deftly scrutinised, specifically during a period dominated by industrial growth and sociocultural nationalism. The development of a new middle class, along with extravagant wealth in the economic revolution, had a distinct impact on the cultures of the existing society. He understood the balance that exists between the economy and the art world by recognising how having a job sometimes meant, in essence, risking one's creativity. On top of that, the economic reality of Balzac's time made him capable of achieving a new level of realism that his crowd could connect to. Balzac was able to humanise social mobility, debt, and ambition in such a way that he emerged as a critical voice regarding the financially driven society. His perception of the economy enabled him to capture the essence of a society where people are motivated by financial goals and treat humanity with disdain while succeeding. On the other hand, his financial issues compelled him to reflect earnestly on the nature of making art and the value such art is given, especially in the context of resolving financial problems. In his efforts to write himself out of his debts, Balzac had to deal with the contradictory relationship that exists between writing out of passion and the monetary incentive to produce.

Balzac thought deeply about the internal clash in his life, which made him examine the connection between art and capitalism in detail. His life, for example, was filled with economic hardship. So, his struggle to balance financial and artistic motives served as a foundation for fueling his talent. Such conflicts drastically improved his art through the lens of human conditions. They ultimately made him a witness to the world celebrating his craft for decades. Balzac's life story reflects his broad reach as a mythos.

Achieving complex endeavours does result in failure and success. The contradictions one faces while trying to achieve success can be quite fascinating. Honoré de Balzac might have been one of the finest writers to step foot in the world, yet his life was filled with exploits and triumphs as an entrepreneur, too. A good illustration is the fight between his help and challenging obstacles in balancing life. Balzac did not shy from revealing some exhaustive defeats mixed with some cumulating victories, which have always been through his fueling hobbies. These life challenges were particularly vivid as he was one of the co-founders of Maison De Balzac. Rather than just receiving and being published, Balzac pioneered and spearheaded the nurturing of budding literary talents, which differed greatly from his other exploits. Along with these feats, many hurdles were more daunting than setting up a business to serve alongside his writing.

His intention of establishing a printing press that was set to produce affordable and quality literary works was diminished by many financial and logistical troubles. Balzac believed that the project he was trying to undertake would make literature accessible to the greater masses, however, sustaining such an enterprise was difficult. Additionally, his forays into speculative bets, such as an unsuccessful mining company, did not help ease his financial problems. Balzac spent the remaining years of his life pursuing these frivolous endeavours with the hope that he would be successful. He often utilised optimistic thinking in his economic endeavours. Still, he neglected that these ideas came at the expense of his financial position. The optics of Balzac's financial condition provided valuable lessons on balancing a person's creative endeavours and their economic needs, which he ultimately placed value upon. At first glance, one would find that Balzac's financial issues stemmed from the juxtaposition between his literary accomplishments and his entrepreneurial failures. Nevertheless, his resilience gave way to considerable literary output that inspired his unorthodox business strategies. In the end, there was no stopping Balzac from spawning ingenious ideas that would correct his precarious financial position while simultaneously enabling him to wield power in the business and art world.

Balzac's entrepreneurial endeavour showcases an artist's immense perseverance on the battlefield of financial independence. The lessons gained from Balzac's challenges and achievements reveal how important determination, skilful planning, and flexibility are to balance creativity and business.

Material wealth seems to be a crucial component in Balzac's work's narrative development. Balzac was a sharp observer of society and, thus, interweaves the pursuit of material wealth with the emotional as well as psychological journeys of his characters. The presence or absence of wealth serves as a potent force driving the plot forward and illuminating and revealing the intricacies of human nature. In Balzac's narratives, material wealth serves as a mirror that reflects the desires, aspirations and moral complexity of the individual trying to attain it. Balzac intricately designs the overwhelming complexities of wealth into overarching themes relating to the burden of financial obligations and his characters' relentless pursuit of social status and luxurious lifestyles. The paradox of being enslaved by debts while seeking luxuries strays far away from the impartiality of solving the economic disparity-stricken reality that consumes their thoughts and actions. Balzac patiently depicts the complete control that material wealth holds, revealing how sudden elevations or dives into affluence or poverty could obliterate or construct the character's life entirely.

Even more, Balzac has blended these human conditions intricately into spheres of narrative art. Through deep probing, he uncovers the instability of desires and fears that often correlate with the shifts and oscillations in one's economic position. Alongside this, various characters' attitudes towards possessions provide a basis for lifting wider societal issues. Balzac covers the economic deficiencies of his age through dramatisations of wealthy estates, luxurious lifestyles, and a life of financial excess and simultaneously critiques the traditions and standards of his age. At the same time, he addresses the all-eroding impact of affluence on ethical and moral standards, interpersonal relations, and individual conscience, thereby presenting the readers with a wonderful illustration of the most profound and complex societal problems he has chosen to tackle - the incompletely shaped ethos of an economically developed society. In short, he leads to a question of the ethics of wealth. In grim conditions, the sole pursuit of material economic advancement renders him wealthy, and the cumulative effect results in the obliteration of all morals. There is an argument to be made that Balzac, as one of the few writers who worked on montage novels, owes his success largely to how these motives, set within the structure of a character's lifestyle, enhance the plot. His characters put on a new layer of skin with each change of season. Balzac orchestrates the relationship between wealth and free will with an effortless hand, drawing social and psychological problems that remain pertinent even today.

Balzac's Characters: Reflections of His Aspirations

One of the most integral aspects of Honoré de Balzac's literary world is the powerful urges and ambitions of the characters, which are deeply intertwined with the writer's life.

Across the wide panorama of La Comédie Humaine, Balzac fuses a multitude of individual personas, all inspired by the pursuit of love, financial success, and social prominence. Each one of these thematic premises stems from Balzac's ardent passion and undying longing for material and artistic success. Balzac simultaneously adopts a myriad of human ambitions through the stunningly crafted personas that encapsulate his literary world, all while drawing a painful parallel to his life's relentless attempt at gaining fame and wealth. Balzac's characters, ranging from the noble Eugene de Rastignac to the tragic and determined Lucien de Rubempré, reveal the nuance of a single ambition to pursue fame in a mirror with many of the author's struggles and desires. These characters are striking in their depth because they, like the author himself, seem to encompass the paradox of virtue and vice, the constant battle between ambition and succumbing to defeat, capturing the essence of the human psyche Balzac so deeply contended with throughout his lifetime. By crafting such humanity into his protagonists, Balzac depicts the human condition and a part of himself he tries to hide, signalling a sense of deeply felt sympathy within the narrative.

In addition, the portrayal of society and psychology in Balzac's novels enables him to create compelling characters who outlive their fictional world and continue to live in the reader's imagination. Balzac's characters embody deeply personal facets of the author's psyche by serving as proxies for Balzac's exploration of self regarding wealth, power, and love, thus constructing a powerful and tautological relationship with fiction. In this relationship, the characters in the novels serve as mediums through which the author expresses his unfulfilled wish for artistic greatness and prosperity and exposes the reader to the author's motivating and ever-persistent self. In this regard, Balzac's characters vividly epitomise the myriad of hopes, wishes, and aspirations, helping showcase the complex dynamics of human ambition and desire. Balzac's character is a living testimony of the author's struggle and victory forged with the overwhelming reality of his life, making them poignant metaphors for the obscured pathways taken by the author himself. His characters serve as an endless canvas that bears the stamp of Balzac's struggle for humanity concretised through the unyielding pursuit of his artistic dreams, showing his undying dedication to overcoming adversities and making his vision a reality.

Lastly, the constant interplay between Balzac's dreams and his characters gives rise to La Comédie Humaine, a monument to the universal chase for dreams and the spirit of creativity.

Taking a Look at Balzac and Contemporary Authors Who Faced Set Challenges Side By Side

Today, authors face obstacles similar to those faced by Honoré de Balzac due to the constant change in the world of literature. Achieving artistic flair in the form of writing in the face of dire financial conditions has been a hallmark challenge that has deeply resonated with creatives across centuries. The life and creations of modern writers tend to surface similar traits to Balzac's life, which was full of struggle and hardships. Victorian England's social life, as portrayed by Dickens, who is often idolised for this work, was no different from Balzac's. His depiction of human life while heavily in debt is extremely commendable; just like Balzac, he faced financial oppression and overcame it through sheer willpower. In addition, the determination of Balzac is well mirrored through George Eliot's narratives, where desire fights off the constraints of economics and gives birth to timeless pieces.

How her literary genius and the economy's needs intertwine reflects the sombre reality of Balzac's story.

Moreover, Elena Ferrante is a modern-day writer famous for her Neapolitan Novels, which showcase further influence Balzac had on contemporary literature. Ferrante's portrayal of deeply personal pursuits while effortlessly weaving in societal issues speaks of the visceral storytelling ethos that Balzac built his legacy. Contemporary writers highlight the struggles that literary visionaries face and, in doing so, reinforce the idea that all creative work is and has always been interconnected across time and culture. Instead of focusing solely on self-biographies, one can look at writers collectively, revealing striking parallels that defy time and space boundaries. Analysing modern writers' unique yet shared struggles and victories provides insight into the relationship between artistic ambition and worldly ambition, the essence of Balzac's lasting influence. This process stands as proof of the unending truth of the human experience, one that fosters endless conversations between creativity, desire, and the never-ending search for artistic satisfaction.

Struggles and Triumphs La Comédie Humaine's Never-ending Themes

La Comédie Humaine, in all its glory, resonates with themes of struggle and triumph that, along with profound depth, captivates, making it one of the novel's enduring characteristics.

The pursuing examination involves the scope of a complex human behaviour set in the epic tale of Balzac's La Comédie Humaine. He takes us through people from different social classes and how they try to chase their dreams in romance while restricted by cultural norms. This involves people having numerous adventures, making mistakes, and attempting to attain success. Balzac skillfully captures the human essence and its ethical inner conflicts, drowning love, and unwavering ambition through powerfully detailed plots. In his La Comédie Humaine, Balzac demonstrates a multiplicity of characters to explain fundamental conflict and triumph that exist in human life, and the epic tale follows the clouded and strenuous life of the protagonist's every journey. In reality, every character in Balzac's book experiences a novel-like journey infused with challenges, which makes them a metaphor for the entire human race. He smoothly transitions from a young dreamer's tragic demise to an old woman's quiet strength and eloquently paints the story of humans. According to the analysis of La Comédie Humaine, Balzac embodies the moral elements that act as challenges in the character's life, making readers wonder who the true rulers of the world are: needs or dreams?

The multifaceted concepts incorporated into the work add significant value that continues to connect with modern audiences, appreciating the timeless 'struggles' and 'triumphs' represented. The entire La Comédie Humaine comprises intertwined themes that welcome reflection as readers gain insights into their lives and society. La Comédie Humaine paints an optimistic picture of the future but shows the intricacies of the human spirit and the problems we face. Readers draw parallels with the characters they follow in Balzac's narrative, and the ethereal bond surpasses cultural shifts, as all of humanity relates to constant 'struggles' and 'victories.'

La Comédie Humaine serves its purpose above all, capturing the hope and tenacity of the human spirit. However, it delves deeper and paints the problems faced by humanity. Balzac blesses us with timeless literature containing universal truths that revive motivation and energy to tackle life's challenges.

As the thought processes, Balzac sparks with La Comédie Humaine, remembering the universal themes of hope, triumph, and tenacity makes all the difference in our harsh world.

After diving into the intricacies of this person's life and finances, we uncover the roots of their brilliance. Balzac's literary endeavours, no matter how paralysing the debts or society's scorn became, speak to the tremendous strength of desire in a creative pursuit. The lust for life and the weight of his debts merge and speak to Balzac's everlasting relevancy. They are marvellous in the sheer scope of their depth and unrelenting love for storytelling and its art form. His characters' struggles emanate their hardships, revealing the internal chaos and dreams that poured life into his creations. At a fundamental level, Balzac's intertwining of economic and materialistic desire not only gives life to their dream but also reveals the harsh truths of life, giving his characters intricate depth beyond the surface. Through this lens, we see how financial bounds give way to the reins of unfettered imagination and emotion, transforming literature into something powerful and deeply real. Every examination brings forward the pain and stubborn valour associated with Balzac's entrepreneurial ventures. It sheds light on the many masks that the creative shadow wears.

As with one's victories and defeats concerning one's business activities, the intertwining of financial struggles and the endless desire to explain some profound realities through scratching the surface of storytelling only becomes clearer. These are key takeaways towards figuring out the modern world where monetary issues mix with creativity for the up-and-coming writers and thinkers. Likewise, Balzac's treatment of the issues of debt, want, and the legacy of the artist's creation retain their relevance today - which makes one wonder how today's writers suffering from such existential conditions approach them. The life of Balzac can be compared with that of most modern writers to help us appreciate the attempt to create a holistic view of the pursuit of art in different times and cultures. This balancing act involving debt, want, and the legacy of the artist's creation leads me to understand the world of literature and the enduring Balzac a little more deeply and how these issues affect him. The way in which he dealt with his personal issues, along with his professional ones, is a great exhibition of human ambition and strength. When one contemplates the details of La Comédie Humaine, one understands that writers do not write for a specific period in history, which demonstrates how humans from any era can relate to their overarching theme of humanity.

ARTISTIC OBSESSION: BALZAC'S WRITING PROCESS

Contextual Boundaries: Understanding Balzac's Daily Discipline

Balzac's daily schedule reflected a constant obsession through which he produced voluminous works of literature. This obsession allowed him to wake up early in the morning or late at night and set out to work at quite an unconventional hour. Although he was identified as a writer during the day, he was exceptionally more creative in the hours of silence. Balzac knew how to take advantage of his idle time by breaking the boundaries of conventional thinking surrounding his society. Balzac was also aware that very few people shared his insight into how critical daily schedules are when unleashing creativity. These daily undertakings that engage in writing allow Perse, through these unrestricted hours of creativity and routine structure soreness, Balzac to pursue discipline and shed light on his unrivalled passion for writing. Because the world around them was asleep and powered by a peaceful calm, the only thing visible was the quiet and gentle comforts of solitude. With a blank sheet set before him, Balzac described the inner mechanisms of his complex works of fiction in furious strokes that set ablaze alongside the rest of the world.

Balzac used sleepless nights to pursue his craft, greatly boosting his productivity. During the nights he worked, he was afforded the silence that would allow his creativity to spring forth and be captured. He yearned for expression, and the night's romance complemented this beautifully. Here, Balzac explored his literary worlds and breathed life into his characters, hurling himself into his writing with great passion. Balzac's datasets show sleepless nights pursuing his craft greatly fuelled his productivity. Balzac did not stop working in the early hours; instead, the morning brought fresh ideas and feelings waiting to be captured. Being able to work disciplines allowed him to shift effortlessly from quiet musings at night to the energetic buzz of a new morning, signalling the strange blend of creativity that marked his work. Through this routine, Balzac personified the fusion of unprecedented discipline and fervent professionalism that created a legacy marvelled at by book lovers worldwide. It is without a doubt that he deeply influenced literature in ways that can be less and less appreciated throughout history. Still, he proved to be deeply inspiring throughout many generations.

The Alchemy of Inspiration: Sources and Influences

When researching Honoré de Balzac, it is imperative to wonder what marks the beginnings of inspiration and where its sources lie.

The author draws influence from vast and eclectic sources, reminding one of Balzac's life, which had many real and fictional inspirations in the form of his life experiences, history, philosophy, art, and the works of his predecessors. His undying thirst for knowledge and appreciation for different fields made a great impact on Balzac in the form of a novel full of intricacies and, at the same time, complexity. Balzac came from a humanistic perspective, a top-tier blend of advanced knowledge gained from keenly observing society. Balzac is known for his versatility and the power to give life to seemingly fictional characters pulled from different social backgrounds. He had the skill of breathing life into his characters, which made them believable. The characters created by Balzac were a play of different forms of art, giving him the tools to craft and his expertise in understanding the human condition, which was step one of the process. Balzac drew inspiration not only from human activity but from the fables of history and the tapestry of different eras.

From literature during the Renaissance period to modern-day happenings, the traces of different periods can be found in Balzac's prose. He was deep within the intellectual use of his era, acquiring the works of Rousseau, Voltaire, and even Schopenhauer. These diverse influences, from different periods and thinkers, permeated his themes and narratives, connecting many human experiences. Balzac's inspiration seems to draw bounds only to touch the fundamentals of imagination. Through creative transmutation, experience and knowledge, the unparalleled alchemy of literature transforms into reputable prose. Balzac sought eclectic influences and succeeded in binding them through alchemy. The prose that followed is unmatched to this day.

Constructing Characters: From Ethics To Endeavours

Creating characters is an intricate process that goes hand in hand with Honoré de Balzac's literature, and his devotion and meticulous attention to detail further emphasises his understanding of humanity. Rather than pure works of fiction, Balzac's characters have the unique trait of coming to life with features and complexities synonymous with those in real life.

From the beginning, character outlines must comply with a fundamental comprehension of their psychologically authentic structure and the underlying motives with senses exploring the possibilities for internal conflict. Balzac and every other focused creator understand minute observations of humanity's actions and how to incorporate them into character intricacies. Seemingly, every character is crafted laboriously to assemble particular features, interpretations, weaknesses, accomplishments, and peculiarities that make Balzac's stories sophisticated. Balzac's characters grow from his words, freely reflecting what is human–complex. Through his characters, Balzac can touch on the various aspects of humanity, such as ambition, love, desire, and desolation. In addition, the characters' relationships to one another reveal the complexity of human interaction and the nature of society. From the multi-layered main characters to the spread-out minor ones, every person actively participates in making the plot and playing around with motifs and feelings. Unique, along with them, was Balzac's gift of giving his figures, each and singular, an invaluable and individual emotional and psychological detail. All of the above develops one exceptional quality which sets him apart, allowing for impactful writing. Vivid empathy and contemplation instantly rise within the perusal of his pieces, feeling the truth and the beaten-out problems in portraying rising and falling figures of witty men or in the quiet depth of ordinary people's struggles.

Balzac's literature presents us with incomprehensible yet relatable individuals, complex characters who are deeply flawed yet fundamentally admirable. As readers delve into Balzac's prose, they must confront the puzzles and marvels of existing reality. His characters, each filled with immeasurable meaning and raw emotion, become a mirror to the readers' own experiences, artfully dissecting the mystery that is human existence.

World: Construction – as seen in fictional reality

As critical as any other aspect of humanity, crafting fictional realities is a big part of literature, and it stands out in the works of Honoré de Balzac. With his world-building, Balzac does not simply construct the backdrop of the narrative; it becomes a primary part of the telling itself. Consequently, he is best known for his detailed and unwavering commitment to realism. Each outline of the structured street, salon, or estate is precisely built to reflect the society's unique structure and France's history in the 19th century. Having understood the complexity of the characters and the setting, Balzac can give life to his imaginary realms. To further enhance the experience of his readers, Balzac embeds his characters in rich and vivid environments that, in turn, elevate the character's motives and conflicts, allowing readers to journey through the wonder of humanity.

The elaborate fictional settings strengthen the story and testify to Balzac's respect for his society. Whether one regards the vibrant boulevards of Paris or peaceful provincial regions, every inch of Balzac's creation is real. It serves as a portal to the multitude of sights, sounds, and feelings. Furthermore, the importance of realistic backdrops goes beyond beautifying the work; it is an effective tool for social critique and commentary. With erudite precision, Balzac depicts the differences, deception, and strife that are so widespread in the different levels of society, challenging readers to reflect on humanity and what decides our fate. Balzac's method of setting the world goes beyond ordinary depiction; doing so requires immense effort, great detail, and devotion to capturing the spirit of the time. Readers are given a glimpse into Balzac's world through detailed nuances of his everyday life, creating an unparalleled urgency to experience the scene he has portrayed, making readers forget the constraints of time and space.

By investigating the particulars of fictional worlds, Balzac proves his prowess in building a captivating literary cosmos that intrigues target audiences across different age groups.

Anatomy of a Draft: Balzac's Editing Techniques

In contrast to the process of writing, Balzac's approach involved the creation of the piece and the corresponding editing work. His unrivalled commitment to uncompromising craftsmanship marked the editing phase. Balzac's literary work was and continues to be a masterpiece due to the revision and improvement process which every manuscript underwent. His effusion of painstaking detail in writing while nurturing his relentless pursuit of lofty literary achievements is admirable. Each draft warranted extreme affection, Balzac inspecting, caring for, and perfecting every sentence, word, and punctuation mark. Instead of simple error correction, his superlative detail orientation ensures that every phrase and image articulated is laden with profundity and detail. His work in progress evolved hand in hand with his artistic independence so that he could achieve fulfilment in the artwork. In the most extreme phrases, every passage could be ad infinitum redrafted until the phrases selected were astute and the imagery used was the most provoking.

In his editing, Balzac's involvement was more profound than just the technical refinement. He engaged with the structure's thematic coherence and the characters' emotional impact. Searching for the effectiveness of each scene, dialogue, and character's motivations, he crafted a narrative tissue that engaged reality and depth. Balzac's editing concerned more than just the sprucing up of grammatical blunders – prose that mastered rhythm, imagery, and syntax to render the beauty that his stories encompassed and cement them as classics. Through his undaunted quest, Balzac became the very definition of a craftsman who paid utmost attention to detail to polish his literary stones to an unmatched lustre. His fierce, unwavering refusal to budge from his editing process stands as proof of the impact of rethinking, reframing, and breathing life into one's imagination. He is remembered today because of the mark he left of having mastered the touch of precise editing and the inspiration he set forth for countless writers to reach for the standards he defined.

A Symphony of Words: Language and Stylistic Choices

Balzac's eloquence in language and methods depicts a reflective determination to encapsulate the intricacies of the human experience in his literature. Balzac's selection of phrases and other linguistic devices is so refined that it helps construct a range of sophisticated narratives that deeply resonate with a wide audience. His prose captures the core details of a story so intricately that it numinously transforms his writing into an art form, making language and human emotion indistinguishably intertwined. One of Balzac's signature style methods is his choice to describe places and people using dense, suggestive and evocative language, which most vividly portrays the landscapes and characters of the stories. Using carefully selected adjectives, metaphors and imagery, he describes worlds with such detail that the reader is transported to the centre of the narrative. The selection overwhelmingly drowns the reader in complex emotions, guarantees enhanced feelings and deeper societal challenges and makes the reader aware of the fragile complexities of a human's mind. Moreover, Balzac's mastery of style includes his use of symbols, foreshadowing, and allegory. These aspects add complexities to the simplicity of telling a story by giving it layers that the readers can unfold as they seek to understand the themes and motifs.

Blending disparate symbols and hints into his prose, Balzac captures the essence of a piece of work, enabling the readers to engage with the prose intellectually. For one, the unique construction of each sentence, along with pace and rhythm, creates further sophistication in prose. The subtle and rapid movement of Balzac's sentences portrays people's feelings and thrusts his audience into wonder. Furthermore, Balzac's choices surrounding the pacing and tempo of the prose affect the narrative tension, leading the readers through periods of expectation, understanding, and release. Balzac's language, coupled with his stylistic choices, ultimately displays his deep reasoning for storytelling. The construction of prose that results in feelings through the reader's intellectual comprehension is not easy. Still, it is an affirmation that puts him atop the list of modern authors. These words indeed define Balzac as a literary genius whose work never fails to entice and inspire the modern audience within the era he is placed into.

Handling outside pressures: Facing backlash is never easy.

While Honoré de Balzac pursued perfection in his writing, he received external pressure and backlash from critics.

The attention of Balzac's contemporaries, whether literary critics or ordinary people, became important obstacles on his way to achieving artistic perfection. Balzac faced constant condemnation, yet he remained a fiercely determined champion and a self-reliant creator. Balzac's ability to withstand such external pressure and remain committed to writing speaks volumes about his willpower. Balzac tried to stay true to his art, which exemplifies the degree of defiance one must exhibit while being stared at or criticised. It was not only outside abuse he endured but rather channelled it as a medium for self-optimising progress. Each of the negative remarks and every display of disbelief became a goal for him to accomplish to retrieve more splendid heights that the opposition was shielding. Balzac's transforming and self-optimising nature of critique stands as proof of the specialist's unrelenting faith in what lies beyond the judges' unfriendly eyes. Furthermore, as an emerging writer and artist, he offers us a great lesson, challenging us to bear ruthless criticism without flinching.

Criticism can be harnessed for development and drive advancement when one understands critique as a constructive element of the creative process. This understanding helps in coping satisfactorily with external forces, emerging ever stronger. Thus, as we unpack the intricacies of Balzac's art, his resilience to external pressures is a beacon guiding other artists on how to endure the storms of critique and scepticism, eventually achieving their creative aspirations.

Midnight Musings: The Impacts of Working at Night

Thus far, both literary scholars and enthusiasts have been intrigued by Balzac's unorthodox writing habits. With the noise and other disturbances of the day silenced, he could give birth to deep self-reflective thoughts that would later fuel his great works for the whole world to see. By merely having complete control over his surroundings, he would be able to produce to his heart's content. At this enchanted time, Balzac had permission to explore the deepest chambers of his mind, extracting the brilliant concepts and insights he formulated into words. His extraordinariness is reflected in the interactions and dualities of his incessantly exquisite characters and their complex stories.

While the city slept, Balzac transcribed the vibrant spectrum of human experiences onto parchment. The silence of night came as an opportunity for him to freely express himself, free from the mundane concerns of day-to-day living. In his writing room, he crafted deeply emotional and honest tales. Additionally, the darkness around him seemed to embolden him, as the night gave him the bravery to dive into the depths of the human psyche and societal structure without restraint and fear. This exploration, alongside the gentle calmness of night, captured the contradictory essence of his writings. Balzac uncovered the human soul, grappling with the purpose of our existence through the lens of his nightly thoughts. The following prose was the product of profound ruminations, granting it authenticity and gravity. Balzac serves as a prime example of the transcendental possibility of night. Countless creators have looked towards the nocturnal world for inspiration and comfort. His moonlit labour has produced works that led to infamy and still, after centuries, live on in the hearts of readers.

Artists become deeply influenced by the collective consciousness of humanity's story, which they intricately weave through art during the witching hour. Balzac's work schedule frequently reminds us how important sleep cycles are to creativity, as his work reflects an admirable blend of temporal circumstance and imagination.

Instruments of Literary Mastery by Balzac

Honore de Balzac, one of the finest authors to have ever walked this earth, crafted his masterpieces with the assistance of a set of tools that made him second to none. From quills and inkwells to writing paper, he used various writing accessories that aided him in completing works of art. To Balzac, physical engagement is crucial as it reflects on productivity and work ethics. He immersed himself in a space that was bursting with inspiration.

His devotion to the mechanical aspect of the writing process is evident in his letters and working accounts. By delineating these steps, he could release the strong bonds between his creativity and the physical world. His body of work serves as a testament to this fact. Besides his craft's tools, Balzac was also able to use research and information to his advantage.

Curiosity and the pursuit of knowledge were trademarks of his approach to literature. Balzac sought to broaden his perspective on life, which drove him to collect vast amounts of history, philosophy, sociology, and numerous other works that filled his personally owned library. In addition, he kept careful notes on his reading logs, extracts, and thoughts. This information acted as a reservoir from which he drew for his stories. As a result, he was able to create rich, complex, multifaceted characters and plot lines, which immortalised him as one of the first literary realists. Balzac was also innovative in utilising and approaching technology and modern assets. Television and radio were not the only inventions he had welcomed during his life.

Along with the commercial printing press and lithography, Balzac was in touch with the media revolution occurring during his era. By embracing these technologies, he overcame the restrictions placed on him by traditional publishing methods. These strategies allowed him to reach a greater scope of readers and marked a massive shift in the balance between tradition and modernity. As a result, Balzac's writings were not only made more accessible but also transformed the concept of literature as a whole.

The tools Balzac used, for example, a pen, a scrivener's desk, and the very paper he would write on, provided him with deep insight that allowed him to sculpt his work meticulously. These tools facilitated Balzac's never-ending leap of creativity, enabling him to dream and reorganise knowledge sculpted by other intellectuals. Balzac's instruments were not simply tools used to aid him; rather, they were forces that removed the boundaries of his unparalleled literary intellect and embodied his unparalleled passion for storytelling.

The Aftermath of Balzac's Work: Impact on Literature and Other Fields

The structure of works Balzac created has served as a guiding light for countless authors who came after him in the construction of prose and the manner he pioneered to have them fully engross themselves in the craft. There is an underlying standard of realism and intricacies set by authors that came after Balzac. That guarantee compels a critic to attribute it back to him. Balzac serves as a guide for many upcoming writers and sculptors of literature as he has set a standard of meticulously crafted settings that compel readers into the fictional world.

Moreover, Balzac's proficiency to blend psychological depth and individuality into his character's development motivated and contributed to the better representation of humans in art. Balzac's writing impacted not only literature but also philosophy and sociology pertaining to the nature of man. A thorough analysis of human realities and societal phenomena provoked and set reflection and analysis in other spheres apart from literature, thus influencing scientific debates and reasoning. In addition, the impacts of Balzac's method of writing are visible through the transformation of his novels into other forms of art such as theatre, cinema, and television. The popularity of his stories and roles is so widespread that they have been adopted time and again, showing how impactful Balzac's writing was and the process through which he created the works.

To conclude, Balzac's literary style shift is not only relevant within the academic sphere. Still, it is also felt in the mass media and in day-to-day life. His effort towards portraying humanity and society will always leave an imprint on the audience and speaks volumes regarding the impact his writing had on society in general.

CRITICAL RECEPTION AND CONTEMPORARY RELEVANCE

The overall appraisal of Honoré de Balzac is one of the most important aspects of French literature history. Throughout the 19th century, Balzac's penetrating observation of society, elaborate characterisation, and detailed narrative prose drew varied responses from his contemporaries and audience alike. In the early stages of his career, Balzac faced controversy for his innovative writing style and controversial themes that were at odds with literary norms. For some of his contemporaries, his rigid deviation from norms and the exploration of human complexity was worthy of praise. Others condemned his unconventional storytelling methods, including his blunt portrayal of societal problems. This reflective phenomenon demonstrates the division Balzac's works created in his time. At first, the balance between critique and refrains of praise set the stage for an intricate and shifting legacy that sparked conversation about realism, social criticism, and artistic revolution. By the end of the 19th century, it was possible to appreciate Balzac's work more and more. It was broadly accepted among the population, and he became a popular writer. However, with his popularity came greater attention, resulting in deconstruction, with their thoughts significantly impacting how Balzac's vision of narration was perceived.

Early Responses: Balzac in the Nineteenth-Century French Society

La Comédie Humaine brought unprecedented controversies to France's artistic heritage, owing to the debates and discussions it incited after its publication. Its approach to portraying stories through the lens of society and revealing their intricacies and psychological aspects in unparalleled ways challenged the established standards of storytelling at the time. This innovation resulted in complex reactions from the public. The critics were baffled by Balzac's defiant worldview, which seemed authentic but deeply pessimistic. Some critics applauded Balzac, commending him for marking a new age of literature. At the same time, others viewed his deeply pessimistic portrayal of the world through his protagonists as a narrative that lacked morality and credibility and was too ambiguous, disregarding the needed realism. The unrealistic depth of Balzac's smouldering creativity also seized the public's attention, who were engrossed with his unique utopian structure of stories and characters that painted an elaborate image of society in France. Balzac's literature not only remained limited to the literary world but also became a part of the backdrop amidst the context of rapid industrial progress and social changes, defining the fabric of France.

The critic's appreciation and understanding of literature, specifically that created by Honoré de Balzac, has changed radically over the years, resembling the changes that occurred in the cultural and societal parameters of the era. His contemporaries spent many years analysing and simplifying the web of intricacies surrounding Balzac's creations. They tried to decipher the many multilayered plots skillfully intertwined with profound characters. Many glamorous praises and harsh criticism of his 'realistic' writing style and the scope of his work became the norm when writing reviews for books in the 1800s.

Anyone who attempted to read and appreciate the literature that Balzac produced during his lifetime undoubtedly found themselves haunted and captivated simultaneously. The charm and brilliance of the human condition were lovingly expressed, yet the complex societal structure of modern civilisation posed many challenges to readers. Balzac's work beautifully captured these changes in societal norms and values, combined with a deep examination of problems in the human condition.

The core of Balzac's work transcended the intricate boundaries of storytelling, bringing forth the inner pulse of each individual and revealing the desperation hidden inside them. The 19th-century collage of cultures and ongoing changes gave birth to an underlying conflict of strong corruption, focus on power, obsessive hunger for riches, undying ambition, and love due to social hierarchy. Balzac's exploration of such themes gave flight to his 'Unhappy' and 'Señorita', which were simultaneously blunt and glorifying, causing deep thoughts to surface within the readers and ponder the intricacies of the fabric of society. Balzac himself thought of the profound societal issues that make us question the grade of moral and ethical standards we have set for ourselves.

Such transitions of soul, mind, and society in the 19th century were bound to create strong emotions. The beauty and complexity of the revolution that followed in the wake of Balzac's contributions turned into fervent discussions in the cultural discourse, where strong and weak praises were showered on Balzac's aspects of his creations. Every head was bursting with ideas, concepts, and approaches, which were bound to create new cadences long after Balzac's demise.

The turn of the 21st century saw substantial technological and globalisation strides, propelling Balzac studies into a genuinely interdisciplinary era. Using digital tools and extensive textual analysis revolutionised how academic scholars could gain insights into Balzac's stylistic innovations and intertextual relations. The mid-20th century was characterised by post-war reflection, which stimulated much interest in Balzac's writings. Balzac's uniquely complex and multi-layered narrative structures meant that he could effectively ensure the underlying motivations and societal implications of his characterisations would be intricately associated with the psychological acuity of his audience. This restructure further nurtured the innovation of structuralist and post-structuralist discourse by enabling new queries into the devices of narratives and thematic coherence. Emile Zola and Sainte-Beuve were key figures during this shift, for they published substantial influential essays that shifted the view on Balzac's work to be far greater than it already was. These conclusions were made in the mid-20th century, accompanied by the greater scrutiny of Balzac's writings, which stemmed from the war. This unprecedented intertextuality, alongside Balzac's enduring contributions to French literature, reveals why these inquiries were termed groundbreaking. Balzac infused his unique style through numerous narratives, meaning the underlying motivations of society were as complex as they were profound.

Furthermore, the growing body of international literature has spurred comparative studies that place Balzac next to his contemporaries or successors, which adds new critical dimensions to the studies of his oeuvre and uncovers essential aspects which were previously ignored. The changes that the evolution of critique has undergone throughout the decades speak to the constant significance of Balzac's writing and, most importantly, the transformation of holistic critical approaches and theories. As emerging scholars encounter Balzac's texts from different periods and regions, carefully crafted inferences expand and attune with contemporary conversations, further emphasising the enduring power of his literature.

Scholarly Interpretation: Many Ways of Looking at The Balzac

Even as Balzac's writings continue to enthral readers worldwide, his literary works draw the attention of people from different fields for detailed studies. Because his works are so complex and intricately constructed, they have given rise to many interpretations and criticisms. Balzac posited the examination of human behaviour, social relations, and some deeply philosophical issues, and in doing so, he created additional layers that intrigue readers and scholars even today.

Psychologists and sociologists have offered valuable insights into the multilayered processes of character formation and social structures in the works of Balzac, which confirms the relevance of his works even today. For centuries, philosophers have been fascinated with Balzac's reflections on the nature and essence of man and his existential problems, allowing for rich conversations regarding the philosophical dimensions of his stories. Similarly, historians have critically analysed Balzac's depiction of some historical events and uncovered the delicate relationship between fiction and reality in his works of art. Also, linguists and translators have sought to unveil why and how Balzac wrote what he did, venturing into the rich prose and strange but wonderful aspects of his writing. The multiplicity of these perspectives reflects the true cross-disciplinary interest emanating from Balzac's works, further attesting to Balzac's importance in literature. Moreover, researchers' different cultures and backgrounds have produced a rich mosaic of interpretations that novelised Balzac's works and placed them in the contemporary world. Because of this, scholarly works on Balzac have come to symbolise his vitality and global appeal, as the themes he tackled in his works are relevant, regardless of time or geography.

Balzac's Place in the Literary Canon

According to the history of French literature, Honoré de Balzac is one of the most important figures among the world's famous writers and one of the pillars of the centuries.

His propositional formats achieved the greatest concern of changing norms of novel writing and offering the rest of humanity's frame within a somatic vision. Balzac's deep tracing of history's literary traditions puts him above his fellow country's authors in the world's literary manuscripts. Balzac's works signify a radical change that breaks away from the simplistic tales of narrative. He strived to capture the complex realities of life. In his works, he masterfully depicts society's capabilities, shortcomings, hopes, and eccentricities. He provides a microcosm of the world through a multitude of characters and interwoven plots. Thus creating his own space in his work. His innovative methods of moulding characters, alongside truthful representation of life, allow him to earn his place among the greatest writers of all time. Balzac will always remain a highly regarded writer. Balzac's work will remain relevant for centuries because he derived universal significance from the specified themes of time and place. These observations of human willpower, moral challenges, and social fabric will always be considered important and resonate deeply with people of all times and cultures.

His thematic explorations serve as a springboard for inspiration for later generations who utilise his creativity in theirs. Balzac's narrative techniques and his place within the literary canon are further strengthened through the distinctiveness of his works, such as his great La Comédie Humaine. This work is distinguished by the fact that its essence is more than ninety interrelated novels and interlinked tales. Such novels and tales serve as a witness to the extensive dimensions of his literary imagination. The scope of this endeavour was truly unprecedented, and the attempt to capture society as a whole earned it a 'revered' status amongst other literary masterpieces, thus placing Balzac alongside the likes of those at the forefront of modern realism and social novel writing. In summary, Balzac's placement in the literary canon is due to his ability to define and transcend time's boundaries, offering insights fundamental to human nature. Through deep analysis, the imprint left behind by Balzac is astounding, and his contributions to literature continue to enrich and stimulate debates in contemporary society, thus making him a powerhouse recognised worldwide.

Comparative Studies: Balzac and His Contemporaries

The dissection of Honoré de Balzac and his contemporaries shows that tremendous talent and varying writing styles existed in French literature in the 19th century. The French literary scene in the 19th century is a plethora of creativity and differs in style and vision. As with other distinguished contemporaries, Balzac's work overlapped with those of Alexandre Dumas, Victor Hugo, Stendhal, and Gustave Flaubert, each working toward a unique goal. Balzac's meticulous detail on the realism of social portrayal sets him apart as a distinct artist. In his comparison with other counterparts, Balzac's neoteric distinction lies within his unforgiving determination to represent Human society in its full brutal complexity. Whereas Dumas's works wooed readers with astonishing battles and richly detailed historical periods, Hugo's sweeping tales of love, justice, and redemption, and Flaubert's obsession with penning the perfect psychological novel, Balzac focused on the microcosm of society and its ordinary people. Balzac's contemporaries are differentiated from him due to the elaborate structures of friendships, the damaging thirst for power, and the societal turbulence that renowned him as the chronicler of the age. While studying the works of Balzac's contemporaries, it is fascinating to observe the similarities and contrasts within the texts' themes.

Dumas depicted splendid heroes and daring achievements, while Balzac rooted his stories in the ordinary struggle of real life, revealing everyday people's uncontrollable feelings and wants. Similarly, Balzac's meticulous character exploration and psychological analysis contrasted with Hugo's colossal figures and fanatical social critique. Such studies serve as case studies to understand storytelling and thematic development in century-old literature. Most importantly, these studies explain why Balzac remains important in today's literary conversations and how people from different regions and cultures can understand his works.

The Modern Lens: Reexamining Balzac Today

Balzac is increasingly being discussed in today's literary circles and critiqued for relevance and influence. Balzac's works resonate with readers phenomenally with the continuous metamorphosis in how people understand life. The 21st-century interpretation of Balzac's body of work places him in a previously unexplored context that appreciates his works for their adaptability while providing a different touch of reality.

Concerning modern psychological, sociological and multicultural approaches, Balzac's works and their overarching themes become more interpretable and relevant in the historical context and current issues. It demonstrates Balzac's depth of thought, allowing us to understand that he is not simply an observer from his period but rather a profound thinker who solidly understood the long-term impact of his ruminations. Also, the combination of cultural feminisms, postcolonialism, and world literature enables a better understanding of Balzac's representation of power relations, self, and society, then allows readers to properly assess the pervasiveness of power and oppression in his works. Thus, the contemporary perspective makes the analysis of Balzac's work more elaborate, bringing to the fore its potential to stimulate debate about equity, justice and the expression of individuality in a society of many. In addition, Balzac's literature can now be accessed via online platforms such as forums, social media pages, and active virtual book clubs. This further cements the aforementioned arguments on Balzac's works impacting other spheres in the modern day. The relationship between information technology and traditional storytelling is undeniably the primary reason why the age-old issues he raised will remain relevant.

With innovative ways of interaction, readers and scholars are empowered to explore and bring to life the multilayered intricacies of Balzac's works. This promotes a sense of collective exploration and shared knowledge. The analysis of Balzac's works in the context of today's world has to sustain the story, giving shape to an eternal legacy that conveys notable tenderness regardless of the era and deeply connects with the people.

Global Perspectives: Balzac Beyond France

As we move towards understanding Honoré de Balzac more deeply, it becomes clear that his influence is not limited to France alone. His works encompass many themes that have captured praise from readers and critics all over the globe. His readers outside France are increasingly interested in his work because of its complexity and depiction of humanity and society with all its nuances. Understanding Balzac's literature on a global scale requires special attention to the fact that his works were translated into many languages, providing the possibility for a wide range of potential audiences to appreciate his stories. In addition to new markets for purchasing his work, such developments have triggered significant academic interest in how Balzac's themes are received and modified in other cultures.

It remains intriguing to note how Balzac's social commentary finds parallels in various regions of the world, which indicates that his work has resonated with other parts of the world. On the other hand, Balzac's literature facilitates international workshops and comparisons between Balzac and other leading writers as well as other periods. As a result of Balzac's comparative studies, there has been a better understanding and study of how different cultures approach literature and Balzac's impact on modern-day literature. Through these analyses, scholars have pointed out thematic similarities, differences and contradictions that shape the essence of Balzac's impact on the world. Balzac's importance in today's multidisciplinary world enables access to a wide range of research based on his works. Global conferences and cooperative initiatives have greatly improved the dialogue surrounding Balzac and the world today. These communities have initiated cross-disciplinary research on the many facets of Balzac's prose, integrating its historical, sociological, and philosophical aspects.

In the end, the international viewpoints on Balzac underscore his prominence as a literary figure, given that his penetrating perspectives on humanity's condition are universal in form and multicultural in nature. His remarks on societal problems and romance are so illuminating that they give birth to new debates and discussions, making him a giant in literature.

Cultural and Academic Resurgence

Balzac's works have received renewed attention and focus from scholars and the general public in the 20th and 21st centuries. This increased interest stemmed from many sources, like the increased focus on French literature, the effective value of Balzac's social criticisms, and the growing research focus on his writing. Many universities have an increasing appreciation of Balzac's novels and essays as essential elements in the syllabi of literary studies, comparative literature, and cultural history. In addition, new forms of research and study enable and encourage fresh approaches towards Balzac's conception of man, society, and history. Balzac's treatment of deep-seated vices like ambition and power and equally potent morality has always fascinated scholars, giving credence to his narratives and characters.

Outside the world of academia, readers across the globe remain intrigued by Balzac's works. Readers worldwide have been able to access his literature due to the extensive translation of his works, which helped foster an appreciation for storytelling. Furthermore, adapting Balzac's stories into films, plays, and other art forms has enhanced his popularity and helped merge literature with modern-day entertainment. Today, social media and other digital platforms make it easier to share information and ideas, allowing Balzac's vision and message to reach a wider audience. This emergence, both cultural and academic, only goes on to prove how relevant Balzac remains today. The proactive approach allows scholars to scan new ways to interpret his position in literature continuously, and when put together with readers from different cultures who appreciate the valuable complexity found within his works, makes it clear that this author's legacy juxtaposes the boundaries of place and time—in turn, allowing us to understand further the depth of humanity and its set of complex stories.

In conclusion, Honoré de Balzac's relevance in modern conversations is a legacy that proves the universal touch his literary work embodies.

The re-examination and study of Balzac's works indicate that scholars still regard the depths of his comprehension of humanity, society, and the conditions of life. Balzac's stories still resonate with readers in every corner of the world, and Balzac's insights continue to instigate reflection and engagement within audiences. Balzac captures the breadth of human experience with great emotional gravitas, as a genius does. His deep sociological imagination of multi-classed characters, the power relations he perceptively noted, and the conflict between ambition and ethics are still very relevant and powerful today. In an age where everything appears to be liquid and social values and ideas are subject to change, Balzac's stories still provide solid support that will not be affected by time and space. The international reception of Balzac's writings demonstrates his ability to write for and about people of different countries and cultures. Undoubtedly, Balzac's stories are shared in many languages through translation and modification, which promotes international understanding and adds to the treasury of world literature. Balzac's books are popular because of their basic truths and show the deeper meaning of life through them.

Further, Balzac's work is continuously at the centre of extensive debate and multi-dimensional projects, even within the academic world. Everyone from the spheres of literature, sociology, history, and philosophy exploits Balzac's rich soil of narratives. In modern scholarship, Balzac's work is seemingly endless. So, Balzac's work has remained relevant throughout history and is deeply linked to receiving critical attention and wonder. In conclusion, all of the above culminates in the fundamental importance of Balzac's work for the evolution of contemporary literature. In the modern context, these writings serve as rich deposits of human knowledge for us to learn from and provide an endless source of inspiration. Balzac's enduring significance in contemporary discussion only cements his legacy as a premier storyteller because his stories have outlived time and continuously touched future audiences, cementing the importance of powerful writing for deep insights into humanity's condition.

THE LEGACY: BALZAC'S INFLUENCE

The Everlasting Impact of Balzac's Literary Realism

In contemporary circles of literature, any prose lover seldom misses the works of Honoré de Balzac because of his contribution to reshaping the realms of fiction prose. In this case, it is important to note that his comprehensive writing greatly shaped his lifetime and literature in general. His works aid in understanding culture, Society and philosophy with extraordinary submergence. In this portion, an attempt will be made to provide insight into the moderate painting of realism in literature, the legacy of Balzac that enables realism to transcend into the modern era. So, the goal is to highlight how Balzac's realism technique plays a crucial role in his influence on contemporary literature. His unique style of portraying life and the far-reaching impact it bears enable one to understand the deep roots of influence Balzac has over the evolution of literature.

Diverse influences in modern society and culture, especially in relation to globalisation, make it essential to analyse the complex society of the Balzac period to learn how novels aid in the understanding of culture, society, and philosophy. It is important to note that all modern literature expert critics and readers heartily accept the works of Honoré de Balzac and consider him one of the most exceptionally talented prose writers of the 19th century.

Balzac's acute observation of human nature coupled with storytelling creativity enabled him to set new standards for reality portrayal in fiction. His approaches regarding narrating a story, constructing characters, and social critique facilitated the acceptance of realism as a genre and inspired writers for ages. At the centre of Balzac's contribution to literary realism is the pledge he made to represent life without idealistic alterations. He painstakingly documented the tapestry of human life – capturing the indistinct and mundane, the noblest of life's accomplishments, and the most heartrending tragedies with unflinching precision. Through breaking the barriers of normal storytelling, Balzac offered a new way of portraying society that was more accurate and in touch with reality, something that deeply resonated with both the readers and other writers. Additionally, Balzac's determination to unveil the intricacies of human nature and tendencies changed the perception regarding the potential scope of character development in works of fiction. Stereotypes and caricatures were no longer amusing; instead, characters written by Balzac possessed depth and flaws and bore a striking resemblance to ordinary people. This shift from romanticised works of fiction to archetypal characters marked a drastic change in the portrayal of people and enabled the birth of psychological realism.

In addition, Balzac's study of the social order and the relationships between the people and their world was so deep that it became very useful for other novelists coping with the complexities of social relations. Balzac crafted social classes, economic struggles, and the entire pursuit of one's goals to assist readers in grasping the ideas of society's intricacies. Thus, his work became a substantial help to future realist writers. Lastly, his unyielding commitment to presenting life in its real and rough form is what allows him to remain an important figure in the development of literary realism. Because of his work, Balzac became a pillar for many writers who continue to preserve the concept of realism, which serves as an infinite portrayal of humanity.

Characters make a novel and one of the critical aspects of world building in fiction begins with choosing the right approach to the character's construction. Character creation is a work of art, which has a lot in common with Balzac's style of masterfully captivating readers. Modern writers following in the footsteps of Balzac think of the character as a living being with goals, emotions and defects that set the stage for the future story.

All his characters had depth, showcasing the intricacies and contradictions of real life rather than serving mere functions to drive the plot. And for novelists intent on learning the craft of character building, there are numerous lessons to be learnt from Balzac’s works. Ranging from Balzac’s resolute Rastignac to the enigmatic Vautrin, Balzac’s characters exemplify the multifaceted nature of humanity. Every individual has a different personality built out of their experiences, ambitions, and societal expectations. To make each of his readers relate to the characters, Balzac crafted them with an unparalleled sense of reality and authenticity. The traits, dialogues, and actions are tools with which every character can delve deeper into their own psyche, slowly feeding the narrative little by little. Balzac's characters are never static; they transform, interact, and respond to their surroundings, struggling with the intricacies of human life. Balzac's works teach aspiring novelists how to approach lifeless characters and bring them to life. Moreover, focusing on the characters constructed by Balzac allows writers to analyse the relationship between characterisation and narration. Unlike the characters, every figure that Balzac introduces has depth, serving a purpose and contributing to the themes of his narratives.

Balzac's characters depict different social stereotypes and successfully tackle themes of morality, ambition, love, power, and other concepts. This technique of constructing characters illustrates how a character can encapsulate broad ideas,mes, and commentaries on society within an interesting narrative. In simple terms, Balzac's characters are best described as multidimensional, which attests to his ability to craft a very realistic, believable fictional world. It is this mastery of nuance and depth that makes Balzac stand out and puts the onus on other novelists to learn from him while they delineate their fictional worlds. Writers looking to polish their craft should consider balancing deep thematic issues like caring, loving, hate, cruelty, and compassion and strive for a universal appeal to their audience by first looking at the blueprint provided to them by Balzac.

Social Narratives: Ideas Reflected in Modern Literature

Today, Balzac's social narrative themes are still alive and widely used by many writers from different parts of the world. In today's world, such themes are constantly utilised in places far apart, such as Japan, America, or France. Most writers today know of and are familiar with Balzac's study of social structure and human nature. Balzac chronicled the societies and cultures of the world. Countless writers after him have not only chronicled but created and pulled through the new world or worlds that were constructed out of the social structures and relationships that Balzac wrote about.

These authors masterfully capture present society's complexities, hopes, and challenges through their works. This resonates with the realism of Balzac. The characters confronting moral and existential struggles along with the powers within society reflect Balzac's deep understanding of humanity and its society. Furthermore, modern authors copy Balzac's sketch of characters and transform their heroes into real people with lives, emotions, and flaws akin to the real world, just like Balzac did. Readers enter a realm where humanity, society, and desire meet in a single place as the story progresses, further perfecting Balzac's multi-dimensional storytelling. Balzac's motives are incorporated into modern literature, and this multi-faceted web of social stories has the power to touch people from all corners of the Earth. Balzac's contribution is further highlighted through the fact that his themes allow him to be relevant to them for eternity.

The Examination of Achieving Difficult Themes Within Contemporary Literature

Honoré de Balzac is the foundation for contemporary literature and is forever remembered for that.

The creation of today's writers captures the ever-changing human experience and society, and this has been made effortless as the primary themes found in his works are adeptly balanced with the modern world. Balzac's love, ambition, wealth, betrayal, and, most importantly, the unending chase after power has motivated modern writers to build rich stories for all readers, ranging from novels to books. His Balzacian works still provide brisk reinterpretation, allowing readers to indulge in the newest themes rooted in his pieces. Combating the endless devotion behind the chase of power, status, and success becomes easy through the timeless perceptions provided by the literary giant, and the sheer complexity of human relations only adds to the strength of logic. Balzac's deep thematic constructs remain relevant to modern writers, allowing them to echo his pieces through speculative fiction, dystopia, and even coming-of-age stories. These works serve as modern parables exposing the depths of the psyche alongside the societal conditions that Balzac revealed. And through these pieces, the indelible mark left by Balzac is sure to stay for many years, not only for literature enthusiasts but for all.

Here in the reimagined realms, readers perceive the enduring importance of Balzac's works, fully realising that his characters' victories and sufferings imbue the complexity every individual's life incorporates. Balzac's examination of moral ambiguity and existential crises is equally important. Each newer piece of work portrays this character exploration or examination in a newer scope by placing them into settings that further reflect the realities of the modern world. The demise of cultural value systems, the moral dilemmas of technological progress, and the loss of faith in socio-political systems can all be sharply drawn from the literary imagination owing to Balzac. All these ordinary yet extraordinary tales woven from the threads of Balzac's mystique ponderings become a testament to our volatile and rapidly changing world. These contemporary speculative fictions surround the core emotions of humanity as reality shapes bends, and transforms the fundamental aspects of life Balzac ponders over, offering a different dimension of reality, one that is heart-pounding. Balzac's influence on contemporary writers shows that themes and concepts are not lost across time but rather cleverly transformed to serve modern society. Balzac captures human existence across reality and the reality of many relationships, emotions, and life in multifaceted ways for every contemporary writer.

Even today, writers continue to pay tribute to Balzac's astute observation and profound understanding of humans by reinterpreting and recontextualising his themes. By doing so, they ensure the essence of Balzac's works remains intact, irrespective of changing times and trends.

From Pages to Personalities: Balzac's Characters Reimagined

Honoré de Balzac's work certainly carved out a niche in the world of literature. It is, however, his characters that stand out and command reverence even today. In the modern world, it can be said that Balzac's characters have served as a source of inspiration to most contemporary writers. Many have taken Balzac's characters and crafted their own versions in different forms and genres. And in doing so, they have brought the characters to life as far more than just fictional constructs. The shift in Balzac's characters is wrapped under the umbrella of his reimagination.

Authors are not limited to using Balzac's characters in historical fiction, romance, or modern-day thrillers. This demonstrates the powerful resonance and versatility of his works. The intricacy and depth of Balzac's works inspire creators to invest their time in working on Balzac's life and character, as the range of adventure is endless. Be it set in France during its revolution or crafted in a contemporary style, these characters never fail to engage readers. More importantly, through such a reimagination of Balzac's work, readers are given a modern portrayal of complex characters. Balzac's reimagined characters can easily be found beyond the pages of books. Films and various television series have crafted these characters to be more visual to appeal to more senses.

With these changes, and if done carefully with fidelity to his ideas, Balzac's characters would remain alive and would be introduced to even newer audiences. The fact that Balzac's characters can go beyond the borders set by language and culture speaks of their importance and appeal in world literature. Modern writers and artists, through this reimagining, pay tribute to Balzac's characters by reworking their intricacies, motives, and relationships, thus giving their existence a new lease of life. They attempt to keep the spirit of Balzac's creations active while simultaneously propelling them into modern times. It can be argued that the reworked characters are testimonials of the vastness and depth of Balzac's literary genius. It is as if they have woven themselves into the fabric of contemporary society and its stories, creating a connection between the old and the new, the deep-rooted and the cutting-edge.

Cross-Genre Inspirations: Beyond Traditional Boundaries

While studying Balzac's impact on literature, it is clear that he works across different genres in a novel and fresh way. Even today, people think of Balzac as a pioneer of different kinds of stories and novels because of the many characters and storylines he was able to create. Balzac's modern European realist fiction or his speculative and science fiction storytelling style are often referred to as key sources of inspiration for most writers.

The essence of the human psyche, sociocultural structures, and ethics is like a never-ending well when drawn from Balzac's writing escape. Writers of this era still draw inspiration from him to make their stories more relatable and complex than simple clichés. Balzac's influence is prominent in crime drama novels, where character actions reflect his works, and in fiction, where the 'real' worlds reflect the 'fantasy' depicted by Balzac. Not only does it eliminate the rigid boundaries of genre categorisation, but the flexibility of his themes enables effortless transition into aspects like movies, books, drama, television, and even comic books. These transformations signify the endless impactful stories of Balzac and the broadness of the subject matter that lies beneath his influence. Today's writers looking to venture into the broad waters of human life are assuredly guided by Balzac's keen perception of the human race. His insights into love, ambition, betrayal, and redemption resonate deeply across all genres, helping writers grapple with the intricately nested complexities of the human mind and serving as a direction towards a goal.

Whether an author attempts to develop a touching romance or a captivating political thriller, the uniqueness of the plot and depth of the characters in Balzac's works is boundless. To sum up, the impact of Balzac on literary culture has indeed been salient, and it cuts across different genres as he is able to inspire innumerable writers with his narratives. The scope of Balzac's themes still complements modern-day narrative, ensuring that his influence remains active in ways that defy categorisation.

The Scholar's Lens: Academic Perspectives on Balzac's Impact

Balzac is not only a prominent name in literature but a central figure in academia, as scholars delve deep into his works to excavate meaning and significance from them. Balzac is well regarded for his influence within a literary context, but his reach transcends to historical, sociological, and even global issues facing humanity. Because of the controversial nature of his work, he has become a much sought-after figure during scholarly debates, as his intricate understanding of humanity makes him a rather powerful contender in the literary arena. Balzac's novels are well known for their complex storylines and diverse characters, making them useful for researchers in multiple fields, including comparative literature and cultural studies.

The literary innovations that are neuralgic to Balzac's work have been the subject of thorough inquiry, from his narrative techniques to stylistic choices. His idealistic and realistic blend has produced countless theories while adding to the intellectual space of his legacy. Furthermore, historians have verified the social, political, and economic life of Balzac's writings and extracted sufficient knowledge regarding 19th-century France and even after. They have pointed out the author's sharp insights into social stratification, power relations, and moral conflicts, which form the overarching framework within which his stories are set. Balzac's work on class relations, family relations, and even urbanisation has been of interest to sociologists, enabling them to draw a line between his made-up reality and the actual historical reality they seek to represent. In addition, cultural scholars have studied how the world is able to engage with and appreciate Balzac's works, highlighting the dialogues that stem from and challenge national borders and what it means to be a part of the global community. This multidisciplinary interface with the corpus of Balzac's works indicates the profundity of his reach and why he has become a point of focus in academia. As with all contemporary scholars, his postgraduate research work led to conversations on Balzac's legacy being of importance. His unmasking insights grant trust in his significance, and so, with every scholarly shift and adjustment, the conversation surrounding him promises to take a new direction.

Global Reach: How Balzac's Works Can Be Found Across Cultures

Balzac's influence is felt in literature around the world, in places that are extremely distinct and different from France. Readers and writers from different cultures appreciate the common themes of human struggle, love, ambition, and societal conflicts that run deep in his works. His study of society and the individual's psyche is complex and inspirational to many writers and philosophers globally. These themes have made Balzac popular in places like Russia, where his works inspired 19th-century writers like Dostoevsky and Leo Tolstoy. Balzac's psychological insights and commentary on societal issues served as a model for Russian authors. This transformed the landscape of literature in Russia and added a new perspective to the storyline. Further down south in Latin America, Balzac's skilful storytelling has inspired writers like Gabriel Garcia Marquez, whose famous piece One Hundred Years of Solitude showcases his blend of Balzac's style with magical realism. This blending of cultures served to create a new style of literature. Balzac's skilful depiction of characters and society also earned him fame in Asia, especially in Japan, where writers strive to achieve the reputation that Balzac holds.

His influence can be traced in the Japanese authors Haruki Murakami and Natsume Sōseki, as they boast narrative depth and thematic complexity by Balzac, which allows them to achieve a high degree of storytelling like the French master. Like Dickens, many English authors have acknowledged the influence of Balzac. Balzac's skill at crafting complex interwoven narratives and multi-layered characters profoundly impacted English literature and storytelling so much that his legacy is still felt today. Balzac's themes and character portrayals also crossed popular culture boundaries from book to theatre and film and spawned new generations of storytellers. Just as Balzac sought to understand human nature, society, and dreams, his work has timeless appeal. This will lead to continuing discussions, and with his thought-provoking insights, he elevates himself above different eras and places. As we struggle through the challenges of the present and the memory of the past, Balzac serves as a reminder of the human condition and continues to offer profound insights that bridge gaps in culture through his art of storytelling.

In Brief: A Timeless Influence

Writers and readers outside France greatly appreciate and are inspired by Balzac's fictional works. The setting, characters, and other aspects of his stories propelled him to fame.

His work has produced an impact that is relevant in today's world. This work has also allowed the novelists of today to express their creativity in new domains. From human relations to society, whatever balance he tried to portray in his works remains important to artists today, proving the awe of his work. Balzac captures the struggle of being human through his writings splendidly, and artists around the world indeed prove this. No other person's life observations, critiques of society, and attempts to understand emotions hold the importance that Balzac's work does. His work goes beyond the staring depths of sociological imagination to speak directly to humanity. The importance and reach of his work can be understood through the fact that, through translations around the world, Balzac's work is able to live through the never-ending interpretations of themes elaborated in his work.

In addition, Balzac's contribution is apparent in literature and other areas of creativity, such as theatre, film, visual art, and more. The ability to capture one's imagination in the way that Balzac has done has enabled him to be the focus of numerous films, plays, and art that have sought to pay tribute to Balzac's undeniable influence. As modern-day authors seek inspiration from his works, they carry on the conventional touch of the universal ideas and problems that define our existence. In this way, Balzac's impact encircles the globe, embracing numerous means of art and culture, which further elevates his stature as a genius writer. Scholars and experts are bound to continually study Balzac's texts in order to make sense of the meaning and importance of his work in as much detail as has been done so far. This profound interest reveals the critical value of his works and the responsible devotion that his literature demands. In underscoring the multi-faceted nature of Balzac's influence, one can fully appreciate its continuing impact on various intellectual fields, as climate change activism brings forth new discussions on feminist literary theory and social critique.

Ultimately, Balzac continues to inspire budding writers, scholars, and creative thinkers, encouraging them to explore the endless possibilities within his literary universe. Looking towards the future, it is certain that Balzac will continue to influence and inspire the new voices of each generation to appreciate the rich themes and resultant captivating stories from his unparalleled masterpieces.

CINEMATIC INSPIRATIONS: DEPICTING BALZAC IN FILM

Balzac's Cinematic Adaptations

Due to their intricate character depictions and vivid societal themes, Balzac's masterpieces are some of the most celebrated pieces of literature. They have greatly affected the film industry. Adapting cinematic works from literary texts has always been an intriguing process, filled with creativity and innovation. This is particularly true in the case of Balzac's stories, which are filled with complex plotlines and characters. The initial cinematic attempts at Balzac's works displayed the deeply rooted relevance of his stories. These initial adaptations, mostly in the form of silent films, had to grapple with portraying the complex emotions, multi-layered interactions and critical societal observations present in Balzac's prose. The Balzac adaptations made by early directors and screenwriters are some of the most powerful in the world. They seemingly revolutionised Balzac's words into powerful images while still appealing to the modern world of cinema. They set the stage for other filmmakers inspired by Balzac's collection. They helped create a stunning combination of films, each unique and powerful in its way. While these adaptations focus on the themes of Balzac's movies, they also serve as a powerful reminder and opportunity for deep engagement with the socio-critical and unique characteristics of his writing.

The filming technique allowed sections of a story to be envisioned in a way that facilitated the viewers to engage with Balzac's world and see the visualisation of some of its characters and stories. Along with the film industry, the methods of transcribing Balzac's works also evolved to capture more of his literary brilliance in a sophisticated way. The primary efforts to portray Balzac's stories on screen serve an important purpose as chronicles of cinematic adaptations. They preserve the truth of his multifaceted storytelling and the nuances of his legacy in the film industry.

Investigation Of Initial Film Versions

The initial cinematic versions of Balzac's work profoundly impacted the author's writings. Attempting to capture the La Comédie Humaine series on film was impressive enough as it was. However, the original work's depth and complexity were extremely difficult to contain within the confines of the medium. The first efforts to capture Balzac's work on film were made during the silent era of cinema. Directors and cinematographers began working to establish a recreation of the emotional intensity and societal issues he wrote about.

These pioneering activities are proof of the persistence of interest that Balzac's writings and the cinema adaptations that followed hold. In the Balzac adaptations, the main difficulty was portraying Balzac's grandiose novels visually. It was common to condense important motifs and prominent figures with the hope that they would be appealing to the audience. Although a great deal of early film production technology and capabilities were crude, these attempts served as the starting point for further works concerning Balzac's literature. These movies established a visual tradition that is still inspirational for modern directors and serves as a starting point for studying the Gleam of Balzac's portrayal in cinema. Moving beyond these initial films allows for an understanding of cinema's creation, innovation, and evolution, the interpretation of Balzac's novels, and the construction of a framework that depicts his universe. This also allows for the understanding of the effortless penetration of his stories and the unrivalled influence that he commands over modern cinema from different angles and over periods that span decades.

Remarkable Figures and Their Portrayals on Different Media Platforms

With regard to movement from text to film, Balzac's remarkable figures have been portrayed on film several times, with each interpretation demonstrating new dimensions of multifaceted human and social behaviour.

A notable example would be Eugène de Rastignac from 'Le Père Goriot,' a character that has been the subject of numerous films throughout the years. His moral conflicts and ambitiously driven character are sculpted as they are, emphasising how well-known Balzac's works are. A filmmaker's imagination is also captured by the mysterious Vautrin from 'Illusions Perdues', and so they attempt to bring to life the depth of his character and thinking. The portrayal of the lives of these and other famous heroes from Balzac's works is deeply human and is done in a way that provokes deep thinking and self-reflection. Also, depictions of characters like Eugénie Grandet and Delphine de Nucingen on screen provide new insights into women in society, demonstrating changing attitudes towards women and power. These disparate figures have been and are intensely critiqued, which is why their portrayals have evoked fascination beyond the books. From the romantic idealism of Eugénie to Vautrin's brooding anti-heroism, the figures of the most well-known works of Balzac construct his powerful literary world still today. Directors and actors have invested considerable effort into ensuring their representations of Balzac's works, whilst modernising them for different audiences, maintain the core of his works and the detailed soul Balzac imparted to them.

The moral dilemmas, complex relationships, and societal issues in Balzac's characters are brought to life on screen, allowing audiences to engage with and discuss universal issues. With each new cinematic adaptation comes a fresh take on Balzac's beloved characters, fuelling new forms of creativity and innovation. The continuity of Balzac's characters across all works shows the interrelationship between written and cinematic art.

Directing Views: From Several Angles, Balzac

When it comes to cinematic interpretations of Honoré de Balzac, he is sandwiched between writers and directors, and thus, his work is reduced to the narrative paradigms that dictate the film industry. Balzac had a very rich literary heritage, and its adaptation came with its own challenges, specifically regarding Balzac's legacy. When adapting Balzac's novels, it is almost impossible not to miss key elements of the books because they are too rich in complex themes, plots, and motives. Even so, the film remains a piece of art and creativity. Balzac's appeal is vibrant even after many decades, and his literary, multilayered, visual works never seem to lose their allure. Balzac's texts have fostered new and innovative modelling of issues. Different sets of creators have crafted children's films based on Balzac's source stories, each offering unique interpretations of the characters and social interactions. When Balzac moved from literature to cinema, every filmmaker opened up the proposition of modifying the source material, changing the time and even the place.

A select few directors may focus on the social issues within Balzac's stories by incorporating them into their motion pictures to analyse class, morality, and human aspirations. Some may focus more on the emotional struggles that exist within Balzac's protagonists and portray the character's psyche, inner conflict, and existential crisis through intense intimacy. Furthermore, aesthetic elements such as the general look and feel of the adaptation also fall under directorial perspectives. From accuracy in period pieces to complete re-imaginings, directors balance historical relevance and modern context, bringing Balzac's extraordinary descriptions in his novels to life through motion pictures and set design. These perspectives not only depict the great depth of Balzac's stories but also further challenge the audience to think critically about love, power, ambition, and even an interrogation of society. Incorporating elements from different contexts, these directors put their own touches and perspectives into the works, which ultimately offer different angles from which to view Balzac's complicated world of literature. In this vein, viewing Balzac through different forms of motion pictures presents layers of meaning that help us appreciate the author's unparalleled relevance and complexity in his work.

What Makes Balzac's Works So Great: A Film Thematic Approach

Adapting the rich and complex narratives of Honoré de Balzac's literary masterpieces to the cinematic medium is an art form that requires a deep understanding of his multifaceted characters, intricate plots, and socio-historical contexts.

His works are well-known for their great detail and deep understanding of the human psyche, which makes them hard but, nevertheless, invaluable resources for film adaptations. When it comes to bringing Balzac's films to life, filmmakers go through various levels of emotionalism, sociological literature, and even stories within stories. The adaptation task is to transform the detail of Balzac's prose into sight and sound to seize the core of his characters and their conflicts. In each of Balzac's characters, he excels at building a universe with intricacies and contradictions that require sensitive approaches from filmmakers. In order to adapt Balzac's narratives, a reader must understand the core relationships, power interactions, and moral complexities that intervene in the story. Balzac's narratives are much more complex, for they contain many stories and even smaller stories. For filmmakers, this brings an unusual complication, as they need to focus on all of the connected lives and fates without losing sight of the original coherent work. It is of great importance to customise a choice of stories regarding what fragments, timing, and rhythm will be used so that nothing important is forgotten and all major themes and issues within the narrative are well covered.

In addition, the cultures that influenced Balzac's novels make them even more difficult to adapt. Keeping in mind the intricacies of the time without losing the appeal of the story to modern audiences is quite challenging. Filmmakers need to authentically capture details of 19th-century France while making sure the story appeals to people today. Adapting Balzac's stories comes with the added difficulty of simultaneously portraying the deep philosophical emotions of his works. Balzac's detailed analysis of human ambition, moral destruction, class distinction, and the romance of power forms the underlying theme of his novels. For filmmakers, capturing these motifs in a relatable manner is most definitely challenging. The task entails internally contemplating Balzac's themes of existence and then externally depicting them in an interesting and thought-provoking way. At the core, the adaptation of Balzac's eccentric writings entails a unique mixture of textual analysis, historical adaptation, and muscular cinema. The task is devotional to the core while at the same time requiring the mundane reimagination of classics. It necessitates a devotion to the source material and the daring to rebirth the fundamental stories.

If skillfully implemented, these adaptations can spark sentiments and mental reflections that rival those incited by Balzac's works.

Cinematic Interpretations and Their Cultural and Historical Relevance

Considering that Balzac's books are essentially a product of 19th-century French politics, one must take into account the difficulties that filmmakers face in regard to cultural context while adapting such texts for film. The films made from Balzac's works offer a glimpse into the lived experiences, political changes, and shifting morals that existed during his life. Balzac's world is converted into film through careful consideration of the details, costumes, and sets, which aim to capture the essence of the period and allow audiences to experience Balzac's world as if they were living in that time. These pieces are also adaptations made as a consequence of the socio-political contradictions and complexities of France that greatly influenced Balzac's writings, and through these, modern audiences can appreciate the culture that nurtured his icons. The history of Parisian streets and salons of aristocracy is portrayed through the stark reality of the vivacious contradictions of Balzacian films. Beyond the aesthetic portrayal of history, filmmakers often add moments of great historical importance, like revolutions and class struggles, creating a fascinating cinematic piece with a higher level of context.

Such contextual infusion not only brings the onscreen adaptation to life but also acts as a link to the modern reader and the ancestral world from which Balzac's timeless narratives derive. Additionally, when filmmakers put the characters' motivations and disputes against the wider history, they add cultural legitimacy and relevance to the film's worldview, which aids in understanding the social climate the Balzac's characters lived through in their conflicts-filled lives. The blend of different cultural and historical realities within the cinematic context of Balzac's narratives turns out to be evidence of the persistent and timeless appeal of his art, capturing the spirit of a departed age while sounding its imprints in contemporaneity.

Audience Reception and Critical Evaluation

It is arguable that all critics and the public interested in movies have come to define Balzac's works and their cinematic adaptations because they have gaped at how simply the films sparked useful debates for or against translating his complicated books into movies. Academics and film students have zealously participated in controversies on specific details of the representation of Balzac's life in the movies and his intended meaning, as well as the intricacy of the relations between the characters and social systems in his books.

The celebrated adaptations of "Cousin Bette" and "Eugénie Grandet" are highly rated for capturing the nuance of Balzac's humanity as well as meticulously covering the required aspects of history. The interpretation of the social and cultural context that surrounds Balzac's character and stories has received praise, with many reviewers appreciating how the films created a great relationship with time and location. In addition to this, the reception of cinematic adaptations of Balzac's novel is diverse and fascinating. While some spectators appreciate the visual beauty and emotional scenes, others wonder how capturing the richness of Balzac's prose in two hours is achieved. Connecting themes from Balzac's work to contemporary societal issues has also received attention with the audience's comparisons of his critiquing in the nineteenth century to today's problems. Additionally, the impact of the critical review on the reception of the adaptations of Balzac is one factor that should not be ignored. Certain compelling studies of influential film critics have created a renewed interest in Balzac's work and increased understanding of his contribution to cinema.

The melding of literature with history and visual art has engendered a rebirth in the study of Émile Zola, where both fans and scholars try to make sense of Zola's artistic portrayals. Zola claims that the critical and popular response to his Balzac adaptations points out the relevance and appeal of those tales even after decades. They remain the focus of academic and public debate, and as a testament to Balzac's literary prowess, they undeniably show the impact his works had on the film industry.

Comparative Analysis: Page-to-Screen Translations

The comparison of Balzac's novel with the film versions of his works shows how multidisciplinary Balzac's works are with regard to adaptations of books into films. This inquiry examines the overwhelming complexity that filmmakers confront in embodying the characters, social intricacies, and historical issues Balzac entangles. A cinema adaptation attempts to provide the original context of the work as well as the novel itself. Balance deeply uncovers a new setting of power that the filmmaker possesses. In the analysis of the translation, an aspect emerges that some ideas and forms will necessarily shift in the transition from literature to motion picture.

The looseness of language and the inner thoughts of 'The Human Comedy' characters, which is unique to Balzac's writing, reveals the essence of these characters and requires the application of novel techniques, film devices, and effects. The thick web of interrelated stories that constitute Balzac's world also requires an economy of words and a careful selection of filmed sequences, which adds another layer of difficulty for the authors and directors. Also, the analysis conducted highlights the overarching complexities that exist between observing fidelity to the text and everyday visual representation of literature. Strict adaptors tend to follow the lines in the book, such as dialogue, locations, and movement. However, loose adaptors amplify styles of interpretation and add new elements that capture the viewer's attention. A novel addition presentation works at mitigating the scope of the described landscapes and sets that comprise the details of Balzac's emotions and the readers' sensations. An important aspect that is emerging and needs addressing in this analysis is the attention deemed fit towards the context of the history within the socio-historical narratives found within Balzac's stories. The filmmakers are concerned with how to render the spirit of France at the beginning of the nineteenth century and the social divisions stemming from Balzac's social criticism, which is offered in the rural and urban and the French urban and rural mark.

Cultivating accuracy in Balzac films in terms of epoch-specific elements, costumes, and settings is at the intersection of culture, history, and technology, the importance of which can never be understated. In understanding how filmmakers render these specific cultural and historical aspects onto the screen, it is important to note how authenticity is balanced with the need to make it relatable to a contemporary audience. This analysis reveals how thorough pre- and post-production research is needed to interweave set design, costume accuracy, and epoch-specific details in a manner that portrays Balzac's world accurately. The analysis reveals a matrix of understanding that spans the realm of literature and cinema and how the two impact each other in the process. It brings to focus the balance which must be struck between the literal adaptation of the text and the creative changes needed for the cinematic interpretation. In the end, the shifting page-to-screen stylisation invites admiration for the primary texts and wonders why these texts have remained ageless for filmmakers and viewers alike.

The European Film Award for Best Production Design, The Honoré De Balzac Award

From the very first stages, the genesis of Balzac's works in film attracted tremendous attention, and since then, the adaptations have not ceased to appear, which on one level reflects advancements in technology and changes in culture and society. Since the turn of the century, many filmmakers have attempted to convey the elaborate detail present in Balzac's works through different genres ranging from silent films to contemporary cinema.

Like many authors, Balzac remains complexly intricate and challenging to translate into the visual language of cinema. The prose and the relationships weaving his narrative are difficult to adapt, and the early years of silent cinema serve as an example of this. Filmmakers of the era had to rely, to an exorbitant degree, on acting and non-verbal communication to tell a compelling tale. With the inclusion of sound and colour in cinema, adaptations of Balzac's works became more lifelike, capturing the depth of the world he managed to create. The mid-20th century rekindled the flames of interest across the globe, and directors, along with screenwriters, started accomplishing the psychological complexity that Balzac's works demanded, delving deeper into the matters of his novels. New cinematic techniques allowed filmmakers to portray the moral, romantic, and political intricacies central to their stories with the attention to detail they rightfully demand. With the shift towards modernisation comes an adaptation that embraces modern sensibility while retaining the human truths at the heart of his prose.

Through the use of new visual and storytelling technologies, directors and screenwriters have reinterpreted Balzac's works and captured the attention of his audience through new lenses focused on ambition, love, and societal goals that are present in his works. Also, the international character of cinema in the age of digital technology has caused the restyling of Balzac's stories across the world by filmmakers from vastly different cultures that provide their unique views and expression to the characters and places of the stories. It reflects how eclectic Balzac's narratives really are and how effortlessly they connect with the audience across different cultures - making him a truly global author bridging different worlds to appreciate his work and the depth of his insights into the human condition. The transformation of the Balzac films over the decades is a reminder of the relevance of his written works and how willingly filmmakers interpret them in different ways and through different eras of cinema. With the evolution of film, it is obvious that future adaptations will be equally fruitful, as more and more aspects of Balzac's writings will be unveiled to charm new audiences and secure his reputation as a monumental literary figure whose stories stand above all bounds of time and space.

Final Thoughts: Balzac's Interrelation with Fictionalised Cinema and What's Yet to Come

Pondering upon the factors connecting his novel and its characters, it is worth paying attention to the fact that Balzac's works have left a permanent mark in the world of films, setting a precedent for contemporary authors.

The shifting landscape of Balzac films over the decades demonstrates a sustained interest in the classic themes and multi-layered characters and plots of the great novelist. Since early versions, filmmakers have tried to capture Balzac's universe, whether in its real forms or contemporary interpretations of his vivid imagination. The movies based on his writings have not only served to foster his legacy but have also acted as bridges that allow the viewers to appreciate the complexities of culture, society, and psychology. Producers, directors, and actors have accepted the challenge Balzac posed in his works by attempting to portray his character and theme and unpack everything on a much deeper level. Through those adaptations, new approaches towards love and affection, ambition and morality, and society and its criticism have been rendered, enabling the public to grasp the complexities of those subjects through sight and sound. Future interpretations of Balzac's works seem unlimited, as do the prospects of his cinematic legacy. The evolution of technology, as well as new methods of narration, bring with them an abundance of previously unrealised possibilities.

From new-age filmmakers to seasoned storytellers, everyone can draw rich inspiration from Balzac's works. One can seek to reinterpret his existing works or even look to modern stories for today's audience. More interestingly, the global landscape of cinema provides a platform for many international collaborations, making it easier to broaden the reach of Balzac's stories to virtually all corners of the world. Moreover, the shift between traditional cinema and streaming platforms, alongside the concurrent rise in interactive media, offers us so many new ways to approach the adaptation of Balzac's works. Exploring Balzac's literary world through the lenses of transmedia projects like guiding fiction novels, virtual reality experiences, or interactive storytelling can leave so many readers captivated and build a deeper connection to his stories. To summarise, the breadth of Balzac's writing and the charm of Balzac's film adaptation serve as the perfect reminder for modern-day readers willing to explore the world of Balzac. The promise to motivate readers through novels, films, and even TV adaptations seems exciting as the balance between creativity and modern technology continues to expand.

EPISTOLARY INSIGHTS

Personal Letters and Public Persona

Balzac's Correspondence

From Balzac's letters to other correspondents, readers comprehend the author's mind as one of the most prominent writers of the 19th century. The author had struggles in life, including financial difficulties, health issues, and personal relationships, and his eloquent letters provide insight into the intricacies of these struggles. Balzac kept in touch with countless contemporaries such as writers, publishers, friends, and even lovers through his correspondents. The letters circulated during this era also illustrate the profound social, political, and artistic changes that defined this period. In addition, Balzac's letters also serve as a backdrop to a discussion of the complex web of his relationships, revealing his life's work and how he was shaped by the people who stood alongside him. These letters also portray the public side of Balzac and give different perspectives of the man behind the moving quotes. Balzac's entire communication is a plea to ponder on the manner of artistic letter writing and the emotions, jokes, intellect, and affection that can be captured in letters. Balzac's letters deepen the reader's understanding of the literary genius and remarkable legacy as the letters serve as guiding materials to the extraordinary author. These letters are enough for the reader's imagination to captivate the genius behind the timeless works of literature.

The 19th Century's Art Of Letter Writing

In the 1800s, writing letters was regarded as an art form that had great social and cultural value. It was the primary method of communication and enabled people to express their thoughts, feelings, and life experiences in great detail. Writing a letter was viewed with so much importance that its creation required severe attention to detail, effort, and care regarding the eloquence and clarity of the language used, as well as the appearance of the letter itself. Additionally, letters were often sent between relatives and friends as a way of staying connected despite the distances between them. As a result, factionalism became a significant issue in society because people were far too elitist. At this time, everyone regarded the letter-writing process as a unique and artistic form of literature that did not set boundaries for a person's rhetorical deficiency. People were able to express themselves unhindered. Every letter was unique, and so was every writer's intellectual ability. The custom of writing letters also made it possible to debate and write on various topics such as politics, philosophy, literature, and even personal issues. Writing a letter also had its value. It was very personal because it concerned choosing the right type of paper, ink, pens, and even the effort a person was willing to exert, which motivated them.

Every letter has a history behind it, such as why the person wrote it and who they decided to send it to. Even the letters themselves were usually preserved for future audiences by their authors, as they gave a glimpse into the everyday life and culture of the writers. One particular memorable tradition from the 19th century around letter writing was that there was a specific set of manners and ceremonies that one had to follow for writing the envelope and sending it. Society was often very strict about what words one could use to address other people, which shows how important manners were in communication. Thus, specific guides for writing letters came into existence that taught how to convey thoughts persuasively and make compelling arguments. In regard to his existence in this very literary milieu, Balzac’s life correspondence is a perfect reflection of the richness and complexity of the epistolary form of literature. Letters were not only a way for Balzac to express his themes or myriads of other inspirations; they were equal to a deep conversation in faint whispers of his emotional darkness and sleepless night-raving rational thoughts. His letters transformed into a sophisticated blend of self and society, intent and audience, where he could explore the unseen depths of his soul, crafting a space within which he could claim his voice as a writer and free his mind through conversations with contemporaries. From Balzac's direct letters, it could be inferred that the practice of letter writing from the 19th century had deep psychological roots on both societal and individual levels, rooted in the need for personal expression and the societal norms of the time.

The purpose of this practice was not limited to shaping interpersonal bonds, as its combinations were also influential in determining the social and historical context of the time.

Honoré de Balzac's letters, as one of the primary sources of his life, private to the large bodies of existing research, serve as a testament to the literary genius's personal life. These letters represent his life, wherein his emotions, deepest fears and even aspirations come to light. Through these letters, the eminent Balzac, who is celebrated for his depiction of society and artistry in understanding human behaviour, exposes his frail self. It enables him to tell his real story; through these words, his self-portrait is brilliant and candid. The letters exchanged with family, associates, and close friends offer a blunt truth that conflicts with the fiction he crafted for public consumption. These private letters allow Balzac the freedom to share his aspirations, disappointments, and the mundane challenges he faces. His correspondence allows us unique insight into his life and thoughts. It sheds light on the man behind the talented writer, making the audience feel connected to the author's humanity. These letters are profound as they transport us into a world where the enthusiasm of creation meets human imperfection. The letters try to show us the man behind the mask.

In the context of private letters, Balzac becomes a deeply nuanced character concerned with love, ambition, and the inevitability of death. His letters allow readers to glimpse into his life and feel they are travelling through different cultures and eras. The letters are deeply emotional and intensely rational, demonstrating how his life experiences guided Balzac's literary creations. Balzac's letters also speak to the fact that he was indeed comfortable enough to reveal his insecurities to the world; in doing so, he shatters the illusion of the flawless literary idol. In the end, Balzac's letters prove his stunning humanity, revealing literature that resonates with people from different eras and cultures, making the audience feel the depth of his literary creations.

Public Persona Versus Private Thoughts

When exploring the personal letters of Honoré de Balzac, one of the most fascinating authors of the 19th century, a balance between public figures and private citizens becomes apparent. These letters illustrate the inner workings of the author's mind, which are quite different from what he projected in his novels and during public events.

The comparison of Balzac's private and public life shows his multifaceted nature. It illustrates the internal strife and conflicts that stemmed from his immense creativity. Balzac's public posturing was not entirely honest, like his private life, but was shaped to meet the demands of society and his profession. Through these two contrasting parts, readers understand the double-bind nature of a prolific writer who is simultaneously acclaimed and anguished by the fabric of the human condition. In addition, the contrast in the modes of communication suggests further themes in Balzac's consciousness, which explains his finer motivations for undertaking the effort to write. It shifts the focus to the relationship between the public persona of an important thinker and their actual self. Aside from curiosity and Balzac's world, understanding the difference between public and private spheres fosters our understanding of the neglect of his life, the brilliance of his works and the novel's impact on the world. Upon reading, it is clear that the gap between Balzac's public and private life is what Balzac's world means and what helps us understand better how a British novelist can impact English literature and plausibly even English society itself.

Correspondence and Balzac's Creative Work

Here, I shall examine particular letters with a focus on Balzac's letter writing technique and style. Commercial featured roles made great achievements which in Balzac's world shifted difference showing many sides of skill and attention.

Balzac's letters are both a means of communication and an art form in and of themselves, displaying his unique control over language and style. His correspondence reveals Balzac's attention to detail, building, and grasp of human emotions. The letter format gives us a further understanding of Balzac's life, allowing us to see his literature's behind-the-scenes and how he crafted his stories. Balzac's letters reveal painstakingly well-figured language and an advanced awareness of the influence of words. Each letter is carefully crafted and full of eloquence and precision produced by a man dedicated to clearly and elegantly capturing his ideas. From analysing the letters, one would see the development of his writing style, from an unpolished form to the refined mastery his work is well-known for. This analysis of his letters also provides a richer understanding of how his voice matured throughout his writing career and the caution and intentions he took in his craft. Moreover, Balzac and his contemporaries corresponded, illustrating how authors collaborated and how relationships shaped their work.

Balzac's letters reveal his engagement in intellectual exchanges, requests for advice, metamorphosis of alliances with other writers, and soliciting their feedback. These interactions clarify the societal conditions during that period and explain the interdependence between society and imagination. The epistolary style allows us to scrutinise with unblurred context interrelationships between his life achievements and imagination and his time's culture and intellect. Balzac's letters further expose the vibes that amass around his works, thus helping the audience locate the real-life incidents, victories, and struggles surrounding the fictional stories. Balzac distances himself from the restrictive traditional authorship and ushers the audience to the nucleus of his imagination through the unguarded sharing of deepest emotions and insights. Such a view of the writer behind the works unlocks a sophisticated understanding, auguring the literary paradigm of managing Balzac.

Relevant Letters with Other Writers

Balzac's prolific writing enabled him to interact with numerous contemporaries, and his letters helped us understand his strive for literature and his engagements with other writers, publishers, and intellectuals during that time. The letters serve as a case study of his time's socio-economic and cultural context and what shaped his literature. Balzac's correspondences often constructed a narrative about the literary scene in the region, which revealed his hopes, struggles, and relations in battles of literature. One prominent detail at the focus of Balzac's letters is his cross-correspondence with other famous contemporaries such as George Sand, Victor Hugo, and Eugène Sue. These instances enable an understanding of the colluding and competing behaviour of the famous literary pillars of the nineteenth century. Balzac's letters are revealing in that they depict his strong professional relations with other writers while at the same time showcasing cutting-edge professional competition. This shows the relations that shaped the literature of the time. Balzac's letters to the publishers and critics provide an important understanding of the real workings of the industry as a practical matter. These letters show how Balzac negotiated, faced obstacles, and attended victories while trying to publish his writings.

His letters detail his challenging journey in dealing with the publishing processes, such as contract negotiations and fighting to maintain his artistic integrity against editorial control. On top of that, Balzac's letters demonstrate his involvement in politics and social events, revealing the scope of his intellect and his ability to analyse the ongoing societal transformations. Balzac discussed with peers the notable events and ideological controversies of his times to express his intellect, reflecting on the socio-political issues of his times. These letters prove to be very informative regarding Balzac's social interactions, complex life, and work. These letters not only shed light on the literary pursuits and struggles of an emerging novelist but also compellingly depict the life, intellectual, and cultural history of one of the greatest novelists of the nineteenth century.

Acquiring Knowledge for Developing Literary Projects and Structure

Honoré de Balzac stands out with a staggering literary output that fascinated his contemporaries and still motivates modern writers. He is a prime example of why literary letters are invaluable sources of historical and particular literary research.

We understand Balzac's conceptualisation of his magnum opus 'La Comédie Humaine' through his correspondence. Constructed as a series of interconnected novels and stories, this work as a whole offers a unique vision of the entire French reality. His letters clearly show that much planning and considerable effort was put into character and plot development. In so doing, Balzac illustrates the literary perfectionism of his pursuits, describing the obstacles and difficulties he faced and overcame in creating his works. He reveals to us the thoughts and subjects of his letters and guides us in solving the riddle of his life, revealing the process in which he constructed his development schemes. We witness the workings of a literary masterpiece and the extent to which he will turn human concepts into essence. In addition, Balzac's letters shed light on his precise literary work and reveal his goal of admiration and fame as one of the foremost writers of the age. The blending of personal passion for novel writing and the essayist's vision to raise social status is a constant phenomenon of Balzac's correspondence.

A deeper investigation into Balzac's letters reveals an author torn between the intellectual immortality he desperately craves and his position within the literary sphere. Balzac's letters portray a clear sense of zeal that resonates with the sheer effort he put into achieving his literary pursuits. In addition, his fervent remarks concerning the world of literature and society at large illuminate his contribution as a social critic and activist writer. Such revelations not only enhance our understanding of Balzac's works but also draw attention to the prevailing relevance of his creations within the scope of the literary canon.

Effective Emotional Appeal: Conflict, Friendship, and Love

Delving into Balzac's letters paints an intricate picture of his complex relationships with love, conflict, and friendship. Unlike readers who depend on secondary information regarding Balzac's life, reading his letters allows one to reflect deeply on Balzac's romances, friendships, and the emotional chaos that frequently tormented his life. The kind of emotional openness that many authors tend to shy away from empowers readers to see the reality of the revered author.

The love letters penned by Balzac to his numerous love interests reveal the sheer magnitude of his pursuit of passion, portraying a man whose romantic endeavours were much more than simple infatuation. His clamouring proclamations of passion and desire, mixed with moments of despair and weakness, encapsulate the confusion and hardship of his efforts at romance. Additionally, his letters to close friends capture in a few strokes the profound relationships he enjoyed during his lifetime. His letters bear witness to the intense fidelity and affection that marked his friendships and reveal the role of social relations in his personal and artistic life. However, alongside the romantic notions and expressions of affection and friendship, Balzac's letters, alongside the rest of the multitude of creations, expose the clashes and strife that surrounded him. From affectionate words recounting quarrels and tensions, the inner chaos that existed among the people further proves that friendliness can sow conflict. This examination of emotions evokes sympathy towards a struggle between Balzac's private life and his public life as an author. Utilising the metaphor of peeling an onion, only through the analysis of letters, do we see the deeper width of Balzac's life, filled with love, friendships, and contention.

Diving into the letters, one can experience the deeply sentimental stories that highlight the furious endeavour for true human connection alongside empathy. Readers set forth on a gripping journey filled with wonder.

Personal Insights as a Tool for Social Critique

While probing deeper and further into Balzac's letters, one can gain extensive insight into the critiques of society that delve deep. By using a more qualitative lens, Balzac's method of observation was far more robust, sociologically speaking. Most letters suggest that he was conscious of these facets of human interactions and relationships and, indeed, socially structured them. The observations that Balzac contemplates serve as a reflection of society and its social relations during that period of his life, openly criticising their good and bad without hesitation. His letters offer commentary on the political realm, the ridicule of the upper class, and the commoner's suffering. It is quite clear that his narratives stemmed from modern-day life, which he dearly owned and very deeply critiqued. Balzac maintained a socially critical attitude that makes the study of his works enjoyable to engage with, and a minute observation suggests that he possessed a far greater imagination that transcended the preconceived notions of the world.

Balzac, as shown in his writing, understood the complexities that shaped society. He explored the differences between a person's public facade and what they were concealing in reality. Although social, financial, and political structures were changing, his letters stand as a testament to the struggles of an ever-evolving society – through his letters, he encapsulates the changing order of life. The ability to resonate with the reader through his personal letters reveals the relevance of his writings and the societies he critiques as a whole. Rather than a simple quest to understand his letters, his penetrating observations on society enable us to appreciate the complex human nature and overarching constraints of society. In letters to his friends, they recount that political order was never stable and societal constraints are a never-changing phenomenon.

Conclusion: Letters as a Legacy

In conclusion, appreciating Balzac's letters reveals his mind and thoughts as well as the intertwined image of the man himself. These are indeed the words of an iconic figure.

In achieving a thorough understanding of Balzac, both personally and professionally, Balzac's letters shed light on the man behind the curtain. The letters are Balzac's time capsule, encapsulating emotions and intellect. La Comédie Humaine is but one of the many effusive pillars of enduring influence in literature. Balzac's letters, which, due to the profound nature of the human condition, artistry and critique, serve more than the intended purpose of communicating. The letters offer an unprecedented look at the strenuous dedication Balzac had to achieve in order to succeed in his career. In addition to that, the correspondence also serves as a keen observation of the societal and cultural trends of the era examined through the eyes of Balzac. Balzac not only comments on his personal experiences but on the social, political, and philosophical climates of Nineteenth-Century Europe, facilitating an intricate understanding of history and humanity. Balzac's letters highlight his adroitness in combining private thoughts with public persona through his eloquent, witty, profound, and, above all, epistolary style. The importance he placed on self-expression serves as an index of the sanity and articulation illustrated through the letters, enabling the reader to find his words profoundly captivating.

The cultivation of correspondence as an art form not only increases Balzac's control as a writer but also reinforces the importance of personal communication in modern society, where technology is predominant. Through his witty and vivid letters, Balzac crosses both temporal and cultural borders to 'speak' to the readers decades and even centuries after, giving unparalleled insight and motivation. In the end, Balzac, the novelist, is praised for the remarkable beauty in the inheritance of epistles; the strength of his words serves as proof of the long-lasting effects he has on many people and highlights the power of personal material writing.

PHILOSOPHER OF THE HUMAN CONDITION

An In-Depth Analysis of Human Behaviour: The Impeccable Eye of Balzac

As a literary realist, Honoré de Balzac was perhaps the most gifted of all writers in terms of his understanding of the finer details of psychology and emotions. His life's work, particularly 'La Comédie Humaine', illustrates his knowledge of psychology on an individual and societal level. Through his character and plot development, Balzac grappled with the most profound aspects of existentialism and provided his audience with deep insight into humanity. Balzac's acute observation and immense sensitivity to detail accurately depict the intricacies of human behaviour, interpersonal relationships, and the relations between people and society. These fictional characters were not just puppets, but they were representatives of different dimensions of humanity – each one reflecting the different sides of human life. In addition, Balzac's stories go beyond the scope of fiction. They provide an intense glimpse into people's psyche, exposing some of the most common principles of humanity's unquenchable thirst for affection, success, and happiness. Through his narratives, Balzac folded in other philosophies and ideas, becoming more of a literary philosopher than a mere writer. By doing so, he addressed the question of humanity's existential dread head-on while weaving a plot line.

His characters strive to cut through switches in life while facing moral issues, personal contradictions, and the burden of societal norms. In addition, Balzac's unique perception of individual psychology and his scrutiny of social patterns made it possible for him to write stories that are still admired by readers today. This captivating lens unravels mysteries surrounding the paradoxes of human nature—ones that stem from the conflict between idealism and realism, between aspirations and boundaries, and the unending struggle to find significance within the chaotic flow of life. Balzac vividly attempts to narrate the essence of consciousness, enabling the readers to immortalise their existential thoughts and etch them in a setting that knows no bounds. The depth of human nature, etched by Balzac's compassionate beauty, embodies each mascaraed passion, longing, and dread and deeply nurtures a profound reverence for the beauty behind the brutally shattered intricacies of our living worlds.

Existential Themes in La Comédie Humaine

Balzac's literary boundary, La Comédie Humaine, has no limits determined by the codes of the world. At the core of this literary marvel, Balzac crafts powerful tales defying the essence of existence and purpose.

Balzac portrays the human experience through a complex web of characters—the novel compromises between existentialism and the human condition in its most intricate form. Balzac portrays complex existential dilemmas and grapples with philosophical questions in La Comédie Humaine. His intrinsic storytelling reveals the core of human existence, free will and the meaning of life. He paints, through words, characters that struggle with their self-inflicted mortality and an innate desire to be free from the burden of existential dread. Balzac's writing invites readers to reflect on their being in the context of existentialism. He skillfully compiles profound themes and universal components simultaneously. The intersection of individual lives and their surroundings is among the most conspicuous features of La Comédie Humaine. He portrays the tension that stems from blurring personal goals and societal expectations while exploring relationships and the struggle to gain freedom.

The characters' bonds illustrate the fictional world and its reality, whose ideologies are salient in Balzac's works. Furthermore, Balzac addresses the problems of morality and its consequences on the course of events in the world. These conflicts are philosophical thinking, where internal and external struggles attempt to resolve humanity's ethical and moral problems. Balzac's approach through this extensive and complex existential theme encourages readers to face fundamental and deep mysteries that alter natural ways of life and bring a unique understanding of human society. In the democracy of Nineteenth-Century France, Balzac's La Comédie Humaine presents him as the most prominent social thinker. He uses characterisation to invite the reader to contemplate their existence as beings fundamentally and struggle with humanity's hardest problems head-on.

Man and Society: Intertwined Destinies

Balzac understood the relationship between man and society was at the heart of La Comédie Humaine. Every one of his characters varies according to them at different places, times, and societies. This is because every character is associated with a place's preexisting structures and surroundings. This context guides expectations that he has to fulfil, which, in turn, reinforces the structure. Balzac shows the multifaceted wields and strands between men and their environments and describes how social structures determine human destinies. This is done through his sharp-eyed observations and masterful depictions of social structure through the patterns of individual actions. Balzac's social portrayals encapsulate the philosophical discourse of self, society, and the self's place within society and its structures. Society and its impacts on the individual is a larger discourse on human life that Balzac constructs for the reader. In showing how he incorporates positive and negative societal constructions upon a particular individual, he shows how each life is guided by unfulfilled aspirations wherein their paths are determined for them. Beyond this, the images of societal institutions or powers in which an individual is contained leave Balzac with an unfinished story of the constant struggle for freedom and belonging.

Utilising elaborate character studies and astute social commentary, Balzac interprets the interplay between the individual and the group and, by so doing, provides penetrating observations on the human condition. His plots are not simply a matter of recounting events; rather, they aim to capture the multiplicity of the human condition through contemplation and philosophy. Balzac wrestles with enduring questions about the nature of free will, self-determination, personal satisfaction, and perseverance in the confines of society through the intertwined destinies of man and society. Since his study of human interrelationships was broad, his appeal covers the alienation and profound sense of belonging that cuts across generations. Balzac's profound analysis of the intertwining fates of man and society is a relevant reminder of his philosophies concerning the essence of man. The timeless mysteries of human nature combined with social phenomena require critical debate and self-questioning: how does one's life connect with others in the complex structure of societal development?

Philosophical Dialogues and Balzac's Influence

Throughout his works, Honoré de Balzac profoundly observed human nature and society. In doing so, he presented highly influential philosophical dialogues that have significantly impacted the world of literature.

Through his novels, Balzac attempts to provide a platform for his characters where they can indulge in profound discussions about the intricacies of existentialism, virtue, and vice. Through these dialogues, Balzac highlights the behavioural peculiarities of people and imparts timeless knowledge and a self-reflective understanding of humanity that adds exceptional value to his writings. Apart from literature, Balzac's reach is expansive, touching other forms of art, culture, and even the field of psychology. The moral complications and the endeavouring understanding of the psyche make him relatable to many readers, and this is why many scholars and artists are still engrossed in his work.

A crucial portion of Balzac's influence stems from his works because they contain agitating thoughts that lead to intense consideration of existential matters through the dialogues of his characters. Balzac's works cover everything from imagination and morality, the nature of ambition, and the collision of good and evil, inciting discussions and pondering, which contributes to a rich intellectual world with no boundaries. Balzac's work has also inspired countless writers and thinkers to delve deeper into the human psyche as profound philosophers, so he has much more reach and impact as a writer.

His examination of social structures, moral issues, and philosophical implications alone has been a foundation for many movements and functions of art. Because of this, he is categorised, and rightfully so, as a world-renowned thinker whose thoughts shaped many aspects of life from academia to art. Balzac's treatment of philosophical dialogues is unmatched in understanding the lifelong complexity of feelings and ethical concerns. The interplay of goods and evils in his works serves as the expository determinants of something substantially important: the human spirit. His characters speak with each other about controversial matters, and Balzac allows his audience to glimpse into the human mind and challenges them to face their fundamental problems and ethical soldiering. It is clear that this blend of philosophical conversation and literature is simply profound, pointing to his extraordinary intelligence and rendering him a philosopher of humanity, making his works vastly and deeply important to all appreciative readers.

Balzac's moral complexity: Understanding the paradoxical nature of virtue and vice

Now we analyse the moral landscape balancing actors and the literary framework of the human story, the strengths and the weaknesses of his characters.

Every moral dilemma in Balzac's work is defined by humanity's pursuits and motivations to achieve their wishes. Balzac comprehends humans in terms of the profound conscience that each possesses and the perpetual balance of good and evil souls. Simply put, he explains the characters from diverse social settings so deeply that it is incomprehensible. This depth of detail and the reason behind a single character is what allows Balzac's audience to question matters relating to ethics and morality as seen in Le Père Goriot, virtue within characters such as Eugène de Rastignac represents selflessness, integrity, and idealism. These most virtuous characters, set in balance by Balzac, oftentimes come through enormous hardships. A veteran with a mingled conviction from the rooting culture of his nation is placed against a world full of temptation that allows for moral compromises. Conversely, 'vice' can be showcased through characters consumed by greed, ambition, and moral ignorance. Balzac shows the more deceitful side of human nature and justifiable Vautrin's actions in Illusions Perdues, which allows for success in worldly matters while unquestioningly accepting the loss of ethics and morals. Balzac does not shy away from painting them with traits previously considered hostile, revealing the depth of human beings and actions always judged against elementary morals. In addition to this, Balzac does not shy away from portraying capitalism entirely as hostile to compassion, painting reality for what it truly is. He goes further against morality and virtue, spreading the claims that set bars for what corrosion of morality is and when one is considered virtuous.

Such intricacies about human feelings and sentiments can be best categorised through this intentional reasoning. This notion Balzac develops in his writings presents immense depth that profound ethics cannot combat: moralities do exist, but they are far too diversified to be comprehended at face value. Through this inquisition, he shifts our attention toward the brutal realities that are associated with self-delusion, ethical self-righteousness, and social contempt. He captures the battle of virtue against vice, which fuels the soul throughout the world, well past the boundaries of Paris in the 18th century. The cross-section of Balzac's literature that we study shows great concern regarding the ethical dilemmas that need answering, and as we expand our study to the last remnants of Balzac's Parisian literature, these issues shall remain when all have been read and done. These issues will stay alive forever, as perhaps there is no other way to understand the complexities of the human condition.

Exploring the Interconnection of Success and Failure

In his life's work, Honoré de Balzac has noted that recovery medical reports diagnose failure and success as common phenomena. Balzac intricately analyses the successes and failures of human activities, and, to the great satisfaction of his readers, he provides complex explanations, seemingly impossible in his times. In analysing success, Balzac describes individuals' particular successes and accomplishments and the rewards and attractions of goals achieved. Balzac vividly captures emotions and detail while portraying the moment of attaining success, be it the triumph of a social climber or material affluence. On the other hand, the author equally deftly captures raw failure. Through cruel depictions of despair accompanied by shattered dreams and dashed hopes, he tells the story of agonising injustices and disappointments too many have to suffer. What brings balance to Balzac's portrayals of success and failure is, however, the delicate intertwining of success with failure. Particularly, he tells tales where success and failures exist at the same time. In doing so, he demonstrates the precariousness of human endeavours. Often, Balzac's characters achieve recurring success while grappling with enduring hardships or face sudden failure after achieving apparent success, thus demonstrating the never-ending back-and-forth of good and bad fortune in life.

This analysis of the complex interplay between success and failure is an analogy for the ever-changing and ever-elusive nature of achieving one's objectives. Additionally, Balzac's treatment of these matters is intricate and offers rich commentary on the human condition regardless of the time and culture. Whereas engaging different dimensions of success and failure, Balzac makes readers ponder over their own endeavours and struggles and invokes self-compassionate contemplation. Indeed, the success and failure paradox in Balzac's novels reinforces why he understood deeply the phenomena of mythic truths that define existence and why he is remembered for being a great observer of the human condition.

Intellectual Roots: Influences from Enlightenment Thinkers

Regarding the sources of inspiration that shaped Honoré de Balzac's philosophies, the Enlightenment period is clearly crucial to his life's work. The thinkers of the Age of Enlightenment, who include Voltaire, Rousseau, Montesquieu, and Diderot, profoundly impacted Balzac's literary works, which he produced throughout his life. These figures focused on reasoning, individualism, and the gain of knowledge, much to the expense of societal views and behaviours, which quite clearly altered Balzac's offering to the world.

They offered the theoretical framework for his analysis of human beings and their social systems, providing La Comédie Humaine's philosophical undertones. Freedom, reason, and even satire, which Voltaire defended and advocated, greatly interested Balzac. He, too, incorporated such elements into his writing to critique the social status quo and the ethical weaknesses of people. The spirit of doubt and intellectual curiosity which Voltaire inspired in people led Balzac to confront the accepted structure of society and analyse the intricacies of human life. The same is what Balzac drew from Rousseau: the natural goodness of man, the power of sentiment, and Balzac's love for human passions and moral conflicts, which made him give deep feelings to his characters. Balzac's social monographies, or the portraits of the modern ruling aristocracy, the bourgeoisie and proletarians in 19th-century French cities, were aided by Montesquieu's separation of powers and his study of the forms of government. This development was seen in the sharp touches of the aristocratic elite and bourgeoisie and the grief of the working men struggling to live in France's urban setting during the 19th century. Furthermore, Diderot's materialism and even his psychology studies provided the basis for Balzac's deep understanding of his characters, the motives behind their thoughts, and the conflicts within them.

Engaging with the ideas of these Enlightenment figures shows how Balzac was intellectually indebted to them. They shaped his narrative and deeply permeated his understanding of the human condition. Balzac did not just incorporate Enlightenment ideals into the fabric of his stories but used them to critique multifaceted society, ultimately elevating his work to an embodiment of philosophical reasoning.

Psychological Realism: A Study of Human Psyche

The wholly singular psychological realism that Balzac displays in his works suggests a deep understanding of the human psyche and turmoil. The author paints a picture of human motivations and emotions through painstaking observation and intense introspection. His Balzacian characters spring to life alongside them. In 'La Comédie Humaine', Balzac painstakingly explores the psychology of each character and reveals faint traces of human conflict and immense emotional strife. Balzac portrays the intricacies of human nature through his characters' emotions. He provides deep insight into the workings of the heart and mind.

From the ambitious Rastignac to the tortured Goriot, each character stands as a testament to the intricacy of the human mind, exposing profound verities and complexities of life. The unfurling of pride, jealousy, love, ambition, and despair are painted on a canvas, and Balzac unravelled them with deep strokes of the human motive, bringing the readers closer to the diverse range of human emotions. Balzac's psychological realism paints a broader picture, incorporating societal and cultural aspects rather than focusing on individual characters head-on. His use of juxtaposition in personal storylines to larger narrative themes forces Balzac's audience to recognise how their environment shapes the psyche. From the appeal that suffocating societal standards norm bring to the observation of wealth and status, the author profoundly probes the relationship between psychological inner states and outer environment. All this sheds light on the complexities of human experience. Balzac, inferring a deep meaning, chose to escape human existence conditions that beg a lot of questions. He acknowledges the fragile balance between reason and passion, the pursuit of joy, and the constant battle of light and darkness within man's soul.

His deep analysis of the human mind serves as a testament to his core ideas about human psychology and the continuing importance of literature.

Life and Death: Balzac's Exploration of Mortality and Immortality

In La Comédie Humaine, death is shown with deep regard, integrating instead of surrendering the narrative to overwhelming flashbacks. Balzac presented mortality and death not as the ending of life but as a truth that every individual witnesses. More so, his portrayal of death is exhibited deeply in metaphors. Instead of simply explaining the person's demise, the depiction is much grander and tends to evoke powerful emotions transcending time, thus enabling readers to comprehend the true nature of life and the dire phenomenon of death. Moreover, Balzac's work is an interment of the idea of mortality; it stems beyond this realm. On the other hand, immortality evolves as a principal theme of Balzac's work. Balzac aims to portray life's grand design and the resources one possesses to attain immortality through art and other forms of self-expression or even the legacy left behind by a person fully embedded with life's importance ceremony.

This idea links with the aspirations of his characters, which are the legacy pursuit and the desire to go beyond the boundaries of human life. Balzac's powerful narratives and dialogues make the readers question the essence of immortality and what it means to humanity. This exploration disrupts assumptions, prompting one to reframe mortality and immortality from a different perspective. Balzac's thematic concerns encompass greater societal considerations pertaining to death and immortality. He shows the transience of human efforts against the monumental boulders of history while poignantly adding to the profound consciousness of society. Balzac is concerned with how the fear of death makes people strive to attain immortality through diverse avenues, thus illustrating the delicate balance between self-interest and societal order. Through his effortless narration, he articulates striking and intricate relationships between death and life, challenging readers to consider the profound essence of humanity. Balzac envelops his reflections within the scope of mortality and immortality as an invitation to question what type of legacy one leaves behind and what influence the actions taken will have.

It encourages us to reflect on the meaning of our existence through the lens of our ultimate fate while pursuing a kind of immortality beyond time's limits. Balzac's artistry, alongside his philosophical profundity, invites the reader to engage with the paradoxes of life and death and, in turn, vigorous contemplation on the permanently resonant axis of every human life.

Contemplation About French Society: A Conundrum Without An Expiry Date

Through the literary work of Balzac, we can contemplate and analyse the live elements that made up the social structure of France in the 19th century because his literary corpus can offer one conundrum without an expiry date. While Balzac adeptly depicts French society, he tackles human attitudes, behaviour issues, and morals and undertakes existential inquiries that go beyond time. The social setup famously brings forth a conflict between self-centred motivation for personal goals and the broader policies to pursue dreams in society. This intellectual glimpse invokes quite deep pondering on humanity's treasure chest of power and wealth that stratifies social classes. Balzac's remarks drew attention to the shackles of a complex social system while condemning the morals and ideology of his contemporaries. Balzac points to the gap between the pompous lifestyle of the aristocrats and the deeply impoverished proletarians, which is representative of the world. Balzac decides to examine the deeper underlying issues, inequalities, and injustices embedded into the core of society. In further examination, the prominent questions of inequality, justice, and pursuing happiness suggest confronting and analysing.

Furthermore, Balzac's fiction brings out the complex side of human engagement and relationships as it forces one to consider the scope of the degree of autonomy and responsibility one has to oneself and society at large. These thematic undertones invite subjective contemplation and challenge one's ethics relative to society as a whole. In addition, as the story progresses, Balzac employs artistic devices of symbols and images of real historical and cultural changes aimed at comprehending the societal phenomena that remain relevant through time and history. He makes such sharper remarks that one takes a step or a breath after having undertaken almost all human acts or efforts to question the existence of time and its consequences on civilisation. This also nudges readers into contemplating the age-old philosophical issues of progress versus tradition and the fleeting nature of human societies. On the other hand, this leads to deeper pondering of the unchanging nature of humanity; Balzac's ability to address complex philosophical questions within the context of French society makes his works create archives of the never-ending complexities of human life. Balzac's plot, characterised by the interrelationship of diverse people, nations, and events, serves as a catalyst to reignite important and principled debates on morality and existence, achingly ever-present among us, as well as exploring deeper ethical and moral questions.

Consequently, the French society set forth in Balzac's novels not only advances literary criticism but also points to the relevance of philosophical problems in contemporary civilisation.

CONCLUSION: TIMELESS REFLECTIONS IN A MODERN WORLD

Synthesis of Balzac's Thematic Corpus

Honore de Balzac's literary legacy remains indelibly etched in the annals of literature, reflecting a profound understanding of the human condition. Through an exploration of his thematic corpus, it becomes evident that Balzac's works are intricately intertwined with a profound examination of human complexities and societal dynamics. His astute portrayal of ambition, love, loss, corruption, and social hierarchies threads consistently across his body of work, offering readers a panoramic view of the intricacies of the human experience. Balzac's ability to weave these diverse themes into a cohesive structure underscores his unparalleled insight into the multifaceted nature of human existence. Each narrative strand serves as a testament to his overarching vision, creating a rich tapestry that resonates with timeless relevance. Balzac's characters, with their relatable struggles and triumphs, invite readers to delve into the complexities of the human psyche with unyielding introspection. The interconnectedness of these thematic explorations not only showcases Balzac's literary prowess but also underscores his profound empathy for the human condition. As readers traverse the expanse of Balzac's literary landscape, they are confronted with a compelling portrait of humanity, where the triumphs and tribulations of characters mirror the complexities of real-life experiences. By delving deeper into these thematic strands, one gains a deeper appreciation for the enduring resonance of Balzac's oeuvre, as his insights into human nature transcend temporal boundaries, resonating with audiences across generations. In essence, the synthesis of Balzac's thematic corpus represents an inexhaustible reservoir of insight, offering a profound reflection on the universality of human experiences and the enduring relevance of his literary contributions.

Balzac's Enduring Legacy in Literature

Honore de Balzac's literary achievements have left an indelible mark on the world of literature, solidifying his position as one of history's most influential and celebrated authors. His enduring legacy resonates profoundly within storytelling, character development, and thematic richness, influencing countless writers and readers across generations. Balzac's meticulous attention to detail and profound understanding of human nature are noteworthy, forming the cornerstone of his literary legacy. The intricate tapestry of characters he crafted and the depth with which he portrayed their inner struggles and societal interactions continue to inspire contemporary writers to explore complex human experiences with a newfound perspective. Balzac's ability to capture the essence of human emotions and aspirations has paved the way for future storytellers to delve into the complexities of the human psyche and depict raw, authentic human experiences. His distinct narrative style, characterised by its vivid realism and unflinching portrayal of the human condition, inspires authors seeking to create authentic and relatable characters. Moreover, Balzac's relentless dedication to depicting the multifaceted nature of ambition, love, and societal dynamics has set a benchmark for literary works that unravel human existence's intricacies. Indeed, Balzac's thematic exploration transcends time and continues to shape the literary landscape today.

Furthermore, Balzac's enduring legacy in literature extends beyond storytelling, permeating into the realms of literary criticism, cultural studies, and interdisciplinary discourse. His profound influence on the evolution of novelistic form and structure and his contributions to the realist movement have had a lasting impact on the way literature is created and interpreted. Scholars and critics frequently cite Balzac's innovative narrative techniques and astute social commentary as pivotal in shaping the trajectory of literary studies, exemplifying his far-reaching influence. In the contemporary literary landscape, Balzac's work continues to serve as a touchstone for literary innovation and exploration. Writers, scholars, and enthusiasts are drawn to his narratives' timeless elegance and profound insights, continually reimagining and reinterpreting his themes in light of modern sensibilities. Balzac's enduring legacy in literature endures as a beacon of inspiration and intellectual provocation by providing a rich tapestry of diverse human experiences and delving deep into the intricacies of the human condition.

Reflections on Modern Society through a Balzacian Lens

As we delve into the profound societal commentary inherent in Balzac's literary universe, a striking parallel emerges between the complexities of his world and our contemporary society. Balzac's acute observations and penetrating analyses of human behaviour transcend the confines of his era, offering a timeless framework for understanding the intricacies of modern society. His portrayal of social hierarchy, moral dilemmas, and the pursuit of wealth and power resonates with the contemporary reader, illuminating the perennial challenges and aspirations that define human existence. Through a Balzacian lens, we witness the interplay of ambition, love, and disillusionment in the fabric of modern life, underscoring the enduring relevance of his narratives. Moreover, Balzac's exploration of human desires, flaws, and societal injustices serves as a reflective mirror that invites introspection into our own cultural milieu. By contemplating the characters and plotlines crafted by Balzac, readers are confronted with thought-provoking parallels to contemporary societal structures and individual struggles. Balzac's incisive critique of corruption, materialism, and the turbulent dynamics of human relationships offers invaluable insights into the undercurrents of modernity, encouraging a critical examination of prevalent socio-cultural constructs. Furthermore, his astute dissection of human motivations and the complexities of interpersonal connections provides a poignant lens to contemplate the intricacies of modern-day interactions and societal norms. As we navigate the multifaceted landscape of contemporary society, Balzac's oeuvre serves as a compelling guide, enabling us to navigate the ethical and existential quandaries that encapsulate the human experience. By exploring Balzac's thematic motifs and narrative prowess, we gain a nuanced perspective on the contemporary human condition. This allows a deeper comprehension of the underlying mechanisms that propel our social order. Indeed, the lens of Balzac bestows upon us the ability to engage with our present reality through an enriched understanding of the timelessness of human nature and societal structures, fostering a cross-temporal dialogue that enriches our interpretation of modernity.

The Continuity of Human Nature Across Eras

Throughout history, studying human nature has been a fundamental pursuit in literature, philosophy, and psychology. Honore de Balzac's profound understanding of the human condition transcends temporal boundaries, offering timeless insights into the complexities of human behaviour. Their respective eras do not merely bind Balzac's characters; they embody universal traits and emotions that resonate across generations. By delving into the psychological depths of his characters, Balzac masterfully captures the essential elements of human nature that persist through the ages. One of the most remarkable aspects of Balzac's portrayal of human nature is his ability to capture the intricacies of desire, ambition, and moral dilemmas. Whether set in 19th-century France or the modern world, the yearnings for love, success, and societal recognition remain strikingly similar. Balzac's astute observations on the human psyche transcend the confines of time, inviting readers to recognise the enduring continuity of human desires and motivations.

Furthermore, Balzac's nuanced depiction of moral ambiguity and ethical conflicts reflects an unwavering truth about humanity's moral fabric. The timeless struggle between good and evil, virtue and vice, recurs throughout Balzac's narratives, resonating with readers from diverse cultural and historical backgrounds. Balzac's exploration of human frailties and moral quandaries confronts the reader with a mirror reflecting individuals' perennial ethical challenges across centuries. Moreover, the universality of Balzac's themes extends beyond individual character portrayals to encompass broader societal dynamics. His keen observations of social hierarchies, power struggles, and the impact of industrialisation on human existence offer insights into persistent societal structures and values. The tensions between tradition and progress, witnessed in Balzac's works, echo in contemporary discussions on cultural evolution and societal transformations, emphasising the enduring relevance of his thematic explorations. In essence, the continuity of human nature across eras, as illuminated by Balzac's literary oeuvre, serves as a poignant reminder of the unchanging essence of humanity. Through his timeless narratives, Balzac invites readers to introspectively engage with the perpetual facets of human existence, compelling us to acknowledge the enduring resonance of our shared human experiences.

Relevance of Realism in Contemporary Narratives

The literary movement of realism, championed by writers such as Honoré de Balzac in the 19th century, continues to wield profound relevance in contemporary narratives. Realism transcends temporal boundaries, offering a timeless mirror through which society and human nature are reflected. In today's fast-paced and interconnected world, the pursuit of authentic portrayal remains vital to addressing the complexities and nuances of modern life. Realism, emphasising everyday experiences, can ground readers in relatable contexts, fostering empathy and understanding across diverse cultures and backgrounds. Furthermore, the tenets of realism persist in challenging the prevailing romanticised or idealised portrayals often found in media and literature.

This critical approach enables audiences to confront realities with intellectual acumen and emotional resonance, prompting introspection and meaningful discourse. Contemporary narratives that embrace realism have the potential to illuminate societal issues and inspire societal change. By shedding light on the universal struggles, triumphs, and dilemmas individuals face, these narratives transcend cultural boundaries, serving as bridges of empathy and communal understanding. The enduring significance of realism is evidenced in its ability to capture the human experience in all its complexity, from the mundane to the extraordinary, imparting enduring lessons about resilience, social dynamics, and the indomitable human spirit. Moreover, in an era marked by rapid technological advancements and evolving modes of storytelling, the verisimilitude inherent in realistic literature is a testament to its enduring impact. As society grapples with ever-evolving challenges and opportunities, the timelessness of realism offers solace and insight, reminding readers of the immutable truths that bind humanity together. This enduring relevance underscores the enduring power of realism in shaping contemporary narratives and inspiring a deeper understanding of the multifaceted tapestry of human existence.

Balzac and the Evolution of Literary Thought

Literary thought has evolved significantly since the time of Balzac. Still, it is undeniable that his contribution has had a lasting impact on the trajectory of literature. Balzac's unique approach to storytelling and character development prompted a shift in how authors approached their craft. By delving deep into the human psyche and portraying the multifaceted nature of individuals, Balzac transcended the conventional modes of storytelling prevalent in his era. One of the primary ways Balzac influenced literary thought was through his meticulous attention to detail and dedication to creating a comprehensive fictional universe. His magnum opus, La Comédie Humaine, is a testament to his ambition and vision. By interweaving recurring characters and settings across multiple works, Balzac introduced the concept of an interconnected literary universe, foreshadowing the narrative complexities of modern series and sagas.

Furthermore, Balzac's exploration of societal disparities and his unflinching portrayal of human flaws challenged the predominant romantic ideals of his time. His commitment to portraying the rawness and complexity of human emotions set a precedent for future realist and naturalist writers. Emile Zola, a prominent figure in the naturalist movement, acknowledged Balzac's influence on his work, citing him as a trailblazer who paved the way for a more candid and unembellished depiction of reality. In addition to his innovative narrative techniques, Balzac's emphasis on psychological depth and character evolution laid the groundwork for the growth of psychological realism in literature. Authors such as Fyodor Dostoevsky and Leo Tolstoy drew inspiration from Balzac's introspective approach, which ultimately influenced the development of the psychological novel as a distinct genre. Beyond the confines of literature, Balzac's impact resonated across various artistic domains, contributing to the broader intellectual discourse of his time. His multidisciplinary approach to storytelling mirrored the interdisciplinary trends observed in the emerging fields of sociology, psychology, and philosophy. The nuanced character studies found in his works intersected with the burgeoning interest in understanding the human mind and behaviour, creating a symbiotic relationship between literature and other academic disciplines. As literary thought continues to evolve, Balzac's enduring influence serves as a reminder of the timeless relevance of his contributions. His legacy persists not only in traditional storytelling but also in his profound impact on the evolution of intellectual thought. Balzac's ability to transcend the constraints of his era and resonate with audiences across generations solidifies his status as a pivotal figure in the history of literary thought.

Interdisciplinary Influences: Beyond Literature

Balzac's impact extends beyond literature, permeating various disciplines and inspiring many creators. His acute observations about human nature and society have significantly influenced psychology, sociology, and philosophy. Psychologists have drawn insights from his complex character portrayals and intricate exploration of human motives, utilising Balzac's narratives to understand the depths of human behaviour. Similarly, sociologists have found rich material in his depictions of social hierarchies, class struggles, and economic disparities, offering invaluable perspectives for studying societal structures and dynamics. Furthermore, Balzac's profound philosophical reflections on life, ambition, and morality continue to stimulate intellectual discourse and inquiry. Philosophers have delved into his works to ponder existential questions, ethical dilemmas, and the complexities of the human condition, uncovering timeless wisdom that resonates across centuries. Beyond academia, Balzac's influence has also reverberated through visual arts, inspiring painters, sculptors, and filmmakers to interpret and reimagine his vivid characters and compelling narratives. His ability to capture the essence of human experience transcends the written word, serving as a wellspring of inspiration for creative expressions in diverse artistic mediums. Moreover, Balzac's impact on popular culture is undeniable, with his enduring characters and thematic motifs permeating contemporary literature, theatre, and even advertising. The archetypes he created and the societal critiques he offered remain relevant in today's cultural landscape, demonstrating the enduring relevance of his work. As technology evolves, Balzac's narratives continue to find new forms of expression and adaptation, with digital media and interactive platforms providing innovative avenues for engaging with his literary legacy. Indeed, Balzac's interdisciplinary influences underscore the profound and far-reaching significance of his contributions, transcending the boundaries of time and space to enrich and enlighten successive generations.

Cultural Significance and Recognition Today

The cultural resonance of Balzac's works in the contemporary world is a testament to the enduring impact of his literary legacy. Across diverse mediums such as literature, theatre, film, and art, Balzac's influence continues to exert a profound effect on creators and audiences alike. In literature, Balzac's ability to encapsulate the complexities of human nature and society resonates with modern writers seeking to explore the human experience's multifaceted dimensions. The adaptability of his narratives across different cultures and languages reveals the universal themes deeply embedded within his storytelling. Balzac's depiction of societal structures, power dynamics, and moral dilemmas remains relevant in today's cultural landscape, providing inspiration for artists grappling with contemporary sociopolitical issues. His astute observations regarding the nuances of human behaviour and the inherent contradictions within individuals have transcended time, allowing readers and audiences to find parallels between Balzac's era and the present day.

Furthermore, Balzac's enduring recognition is evident in the myriad adaptations of his work in other creative forms. Balzac's influence pervades multiple artistic domains, whether it is through reinterpretations in theatre productions, reimaginings in cinematic adaptations, or inspiration for visual artists seeking to capture the spirit of his narratives. The preservation of his characters and themes in these diverse modes of expression underscores his storytelling's enduring relevance and richness. Beyond the realm of arts and culture, Balzac's profound insights into the complexities of human psychology and social interactions have also permeated academic discourse. Scholars and intellectuals continue to delve into the depths of Balzac's narrative oeuvre, dissecting its implications for understanding historical contexts, literary theory, and socio-cultural perspectives. His multidimensional characters and intricate plotlines offer fertile ground for academic exploration, fostering critical dialogues extending far beyond traditional literary analysis's confines. As such, Balzac's cultural significance and recognition today extend beyond mere literary appreciation, embodying a multifaceted tapestry of influence that spans artistic creation, critical inquiry, and societal reflection. His narratives continue to inform and inspire, inviting new generations to engage with the timeless questions and profound observations that form the cornerstone of his literary contributions.

Concluding Insights into Balzac's Human Philosophy

As we delve deeper into Balzac's literary oeuvre, it becomes increasingly evident that his works transcend time and remain inexorably intertwined with the essence of human existence. Within this profundity, one uncovers the crux of Balzac's human philosophy. The celebrated author's keen insight into the intricacies of human nature is encapsulated in his portrayal of characters from diverse social strata, each representing a unique facet of the human condition. By masterfully weaving narrative tapestries that depict the full spectrum of human emotions, ambitions, and follies, Balzac transcends the temporal confines of his era, offering timeless reflections on the universal truths that define our being. His profound understanding of the human psyche resonates deeply, serving as an eternal wellspring of wisdom for readers across generations. Through his works, Balzac invites introspection and contemplation, challenging us to confront fundamental questions about morality, desire, societal constructs, and the pursuit of happiness. His human philosophy unveils the intricate balance between noble aspirations and inherent flaws that shape the human experience. Moreover, Balzac's nuanced exploration of relationships, power dynamics, and the relentless pursuit of material wealth draws attention to the perennial themes that continue reverberating in contemporary society. Through his acute observations and uncanny ability to capture the complexity of human interactions, Balzac imparts enduring lessons that provide profound insights into the multifaceted nature of human existence. His human philosophy, steeped in astute observations and empathetic portrayals, serves as a guiding light, illuminating the labyrinthine passages of our collective consciousness. In conclusion, Balzac's human philosophy endures as a testament to the timelessness of his literary contributions, inviting us to navigate through the intricate tapestry of human existence with empathy, understanding, and a resolute commitment to unravelling the enigmatic truths that bind us all.

Final Thoughts: Bridging Past and Present

As we conclude this exploration of Honoré de Balzac's literary legacy, it becomes evident that his insights into the human condition remain timeless, offering profound relevance in our modern world. His keen observations of society, interpersonal relationships, and the complexities of ambition and morality resonate with contemporary readers, drawing poignant parallels between the tumultuous realities of Balzac's era and the nuances of our present-day existence. Bridging past and present, Balzac's narratives mirror the enduring qualities and dilemmas of humanity. Through his penetrating character studies and intricate plotlines, he delves deep into the intricacies of human nature, unravelling the timeless threads that bind individuals across generations. The themes of love, betrayal, ambition, and societal dynamics portrayed in Balzac's works provide invaluable insight into the universal experiences that transcend temporal boundaries. By bridging past and present, we realise that the human spirit's fundamental aspects persist, regardless of the evolving landscapes of culture, technology, and societal norms. In contemplating Balzac's novels, a striking continuity of emotions and motivations continues to shape our interactions and aspirations in the present day.

Furthermore, by studying Balzac's narratives, we engage in an ongoing dialogue with history, gaining a deeper understanding of the evolution and perpetuation of human values, aspirations, and flaws. This symbiotic exchange between past and present amplifies the significance of Balzac's literary contributions, enriching our perception of the timeless resilience and frailties inherent in the human experience. Additionally, through the lens of Balzac's remarkable oeuvre, we are encouraged to reflect on the enduring influence of realism in contemporary storytelling. Despite the ever-changing tides of literary trends, the enduring allure of authentic representation and profound psychological depth, as championed by Balzac, offers a compelling bridge to connect historical, literary movements with modern creative expressions. By examining Balzac's impact on literary thought, we unveil the enduring relevance of his narrative techniques and thematic explorations, laying the foundation for a deeper appreciation of the evolution of storytelling from the 19th century to the present day. As we navigate these reflections, it becomes unmistakably clear that Balzac's profound understanding of the human psyche and its intricate relationship with society transcends time constraints, continuing to inspire and provoke contemplation in our contemporary cultural landscape. In essence, Balzac's legacy serves as a bridge that unites the enduring elements of human nature across epochs, inviting readers to embark on an enriching journey that seamlessly traverses the tapestries of time.

Selected Bibliography

Balzac's Works:

SCÈNES DE LA VIE PRIVÉE : La Maison du chat-qui-pelote · Le Bal de Sceaux · La Bourse · La Vendetta · Madame Firmiani · Une double famille · La Paix du ménage · La Fausse Maîtresse · Etude de femme · Albert Savarus ·Mémoires de deux jeunes mariées · Une fille d'Ève · La Femme abandonnée · La Grenadière · Le Message · Gobseck · Autre étude de femme · La Femme de trente ans · Le Père Goriot · Le Colonel Chabert · Le Contrat de mariage · La Messe de l'athée · Béatrix · La Grande Bretèche · Modeste Mignon · Honorine · Un début dans la vie

SCÈNES DE LA VIE DE PROVINCE : Ursule Mirouët · Eugénie Grandet · Pierrette · Le Curé de Tours · La Rabouilleuse · L'Illustre Gaudissart · La Muse du département · Le Lys dans la vallée · Illusions perdues : Les Deux Poètes – Un grand homme de province à Paris – Les souffrances de l'inventeur (Ève et David) · La Vieille Fille · Le Cabinet des Antiques

SCÈNES DE LA VIE PARISIENNE : Histoire des Treize : Ferragus – La Duchesse de Langeais – La Fille aux yeux d'or · Facino Cane · Sarrasine · L'Interdiction · César Birotteau ·La Maison Nucingen ·Pierre Grassou · Les Secrets de la princesse de Cadignan · Les Employés ou la Femme supérieure · Splendeurs et misères des courtisanes · Les Parents pauvres : La Cousine Bette – Le Cousin Pons· Un prince de la bohème · Un homme d'affaires · Gaudissart II · Les Comédiens sans le savoir · Les Petits Bourgeois · L'Envers de l'histoire contemporaine

SCÈNES DE LA VIE POLITIQUE : Un épisode sous la Terreur · Une ténébreuse affaire · Le Député d'Arcis · Z. Marcas

SCÈNES DE LA VIE MILITAIRE : Les Chouans · Une passion dans le désert

SCÈNES DE LA VIE DE CAMPAGNE : Les Paysans · Le Médecin de campagne · Le Curé de village

ETUDES PHILOSOPHIQUES : La Peau de chagrin · Jésus-Christ en Flandre · Melmoth réconcilié · Le Chef-d'œuvre inconnu · La Recherche de l'absolu · Massimilla Doni · Gambara · Les Proscrits · Louis Lambert · Séraphîta · L'Enfant maudit · Les Marana · Adieu ! · Le Réquisitionnaire · El Verdugo · Un drame au bord de la mer · L'Auberge rouge · L'Élixir de longue vie · Maître Cornélius · Sur Catherine de Médicis

ETUDES ANALYTIQUES : Physiologie du mariage · Petites Misères de la vie conjugale · Pathologie de la vie sociale : Traité de la vie élégante – Théorie de la démarche – Traité des excitants modernes

CONTES et ESSAIS : Les contes bruns · Contes drolatiques · Code des gens honnêtes · Le notaire · Une rue de Paris et son habitant · Tony sans soin · Un partage qui coûte cher · L'ours et le bûcheron · Fleurette

OEUVRES THÉÂTRALES : Vautrin · Les ressources de Quinola · Paméla Giraud · La marâtre· Le faiseur (Mercadet)

On Balzac

The most influential French critical works on Balzac and La Comédie humaine focus on various aspects of his work, including his realism, his social satire, and his influence on other art forms.

Realism and Social Satire

Balzac is recognised as a master of critical realism, using La Comédie humaine to reflect French social life in the early 1800s. His work is often seen as social satire, where he constructs ideal types to represent the different social classes of his time. This approach is exemplified in works such as 'César Birotteau', which, despite criticism of its length and detail, is considered central to La Comédie humaine.

Influence on Film and Literature

Balzac also influenced the cinema, notably through French New Wave directors such as Éric Rohmer and Jacques Rivette, who applied Balzacian principles to their cinematic practice. François Truffaut also used La Comédie humaine as a model for his cinematic innovations, particularly in his series of autobiographical films about Antoine Doinel.

Literary criticism and analysis

Literary critics such as Henry James have explored the critical links between Balzac and other literary movements, although James has sometimes misinterpreted Balzac as pseudo-decadent. Recent studies continue to explore the complexity of Balzac's work, highlighting his role as a social chronicler and his lasting influence on literature and culture.

Conclusion

In summary, French criticism of Balzac and La Comédie humaine highlights his role as a pioneer of realism, his ability to capture the French society of his time, and his influence on other art forms. These works highlight the richness and complexity of his work, which continues to inspire and provoke critical debate.

- Abele, C. (2023). Generating Life from Literature: Proust in Balzac's Aquarium. Dix-Neuf, 27, 286 - 301. https://doi.org/10.1080/14787318.2023.2228146.
- Auer, M. (2010). Inter-Titles and Calendar-Time: Godard's History of Manners. Quarterly Review of Film and Video, 28, 1 - 12. https://doi.org/10.1080/10509200802433079.
- Balzac, H. de (1843). *La Comédie humaine*. Éditions Garnier.
- Balthus. (1978). *La lettre à Balzac*. Paris, France : Éditions de la Différence.

- Beebe, M. (1960). The Lesson of Balzac's Artists. Criticism, 2, 1.
- Berler, L. (1996). *La philosophie dans l'œuvre de Balzac.* Paris, France : Éditions L'Harmattan.
- Bottin, M. (2003). *L'art de la narration chez Balzac.* Paris, France : Éditions Albin Michel.
- Bourget, P. (1910). *Études et portraits.* Paris, France : Éditions Bernard Grasset.
- Bourdon, É. (1998). *Balzac en son temps.* Paris, France : Éditions Klincksieck.
- Braud, E. (2005). *Balzac et le réalisme.* Paris, France: Éditions Champion.
- Brooks, P. (2022). Honoré de Balzac. https://doi.org/10.1093/oso/9780192846709.001.0001.
- Chardonne, R. (1945). *Balzac, l'homme et le style.* Paris, France : Éditions Grasset.
- Dina, J. (2017). *Balzac et le monde moderne.* Paris, France : Éditions Naïve.
- Dosteïevski, F. (1965). *Les Frères Karamazov.* Éditions Gallimard. (Réflexions sur Balzac).
- Faucher, D. (2019). *Le mythe de Balzac dans la culture contemporaine.* Paris, France : Éditions Anacharsis.
- Fang, J. (2009). Yang Changlong's Dissemination of "Balzac". Journal of Shaoyang University.
- Galeno, A., & Castro, G. (2022). Balzac and the Literature of Complexity. Global Journal of Human-Social Science. https://doi.org/10.34257/gjhssavol22is6pg1.
- Gelmini, L. (2018). Balzac: An Artist and an Entrepreneur. Journal of Social Science Studies, 4, 1. https://doi.org/10.20849/ajsss.v4i1.538.
- Greene, J. (2022). Dealing and Collecting in Balzac's Last Novel. Mouvances Francophones. https://doi.org/10.5206/mf.v7i1.15480.
- Hayward, M. (2001). The myth of Balzac's mysticism: his father's mesmerist ideals. History of European Ideas, 27, 273 - 287. https://doi.org/10.1016/S0191-6599(01)00049-3.

- Heathcote, O. (2009). Balzac and Theory, Balzac as Theory. Paragraph, 32, 197-213. https://doi.org/10.3366/E0264833409000534.
- Heathcote, O. (2010). Honoré de Balzac. French Studies: A Quarterly Review, 64, 463 - 470. https://doi.org/10.1093/fs/knq107.
- Hua, F. (2003). Artistic Figures Created by Balzac. Journal of Pingyuan University.
- Kai-Hua, C. (2009). Commendation on Balzac by Marks and Engels. Journal of Shaoyang University.
- Kanes, M. (1976). Balzac's Comedy of Words. https://doi.org/10.1515/9781400869695.
- Knight, D. (2018). The Cambridge Companion to Balzac ed. by Owen Heathcote and Andrew Watts (review). French Studies: A Quarterly Review, 72, 118 - 118.
- Labio, C. (2012). Balzac: Une Éthique de la description (review). Nineteenth-Century French Studies, 40, 337 - 338. https://doi.org/10.1353/NCF.2012.0005.
- Lazare, B. (1999). *Balzac et le roman moderne*. Paris, France : Presses Universitaires de France.
- La Bruyère, J. de (2010). *Pensées, caractères*. Paris, France : Éditions Le Livre de Poche. (Analyse de la morale balzacienne).
- Moulin, T. (2013). Doctors in Balzac's work. Frontiers of neurology and neuroscience, 31, 225-35. https://doi.org/10.1159/000343671.
- Moccia, M. (2017). Balzac peint les français: social satire and construction of ideal types in Les français peints par eux-mêmes. Between, 6. https://doi.org/10.13125/2039-6597/1529.
- Perciaccante, A., Riva, M., Coralli, A., Charlier, P., & Bianucci, R. (2016). The Death of Balzac (1799-1850) and the Treatment of Heart Failure During the Nineteenth Century. Journal of cardiac failure, 22 11, 930-933. https://doi.org/10.1016/j.cardfail.2016.09.005.

- Proust, M. (1954). *Contre Sainte-Beuve*. Paris, France : Éditions Plon. (Réflexions sur Balzac).
- Robb, G. (1946). Balzac: A Biography.
- Shuh, R. (2001). Madness and Military History in Balzac's "Adieu". French Forum, 26, 39 - 51. https://doi.org/10.1353/FRF.2001.0011.
- Simenon, G. (1961). *Balzac*. Paris, France : Éditions des Deux Terres.
- Stanfield, P. (1988). Yeats and Balzac. https://doi.org/10.1007/978-1-349-18964-9_5.
- Thibaudet, A. (1944). *La Critique littéraire de Balzac*. Paris, France : Éditions José Corti.
- Tilby, M. (2012). Honoré de Balzac (1799–1850): 'Realism' and authority. https://doi.org/10.1017/CCOL9780521515047.013.
- Ulloa, J. (2017). El espacio parisino en Pére Goriot de Balzac.
- Valentine, C. (2020). Not Noticing, Infallibly: The Critical Liaisons of Henry James, French Decadence, and Honoré de Balzac. The Henry James Review, 41, 115 - 97. https://doi.org/10.1353/hjr.2020.0012.
- Vareille, A. (2005). « C'est la vie qui exagère » : quelques remarques à propos de la mort de Balzac dans « La 628- E8 » d'Octave Mirbeau.
- White, J. (2016). Balzac: A Socio-Material Archaeology of Paris, 147-163. https://doi.org/10.1057/978-1-137-54911-2_9.
- Young, P. (2019). 'Je fus blessé par Napoléon: César Birotteau's Ambiguous Claim to Fame'. Dix-Neuf, 23, 103 - 90. https://doi.org/10.1080/14787318.2019.1624013.
- Zea, Z. (2019). Balzac Reframed: The Classical and Modern Faces of Éric Rohmer and Jacques Rivette. https://doi.org/10.1007/978-3-030-30615-1.

www.ingramcontent.com/pod-product-compliance
Lightning Source LLC
Chambersburg PA
CBHW061152210726
48294CB00006B/1653
* 9 7 8 1 7 8 7 9 5 1 5 7 0 *